WHAT MUST I DO TO BE SAVED?

Also by William P. Grady:

*FINAL AUTHORITY: A Christian's
Guide to the King James Bible*

*WHAT HATH GOD WROUGHT!: A Biblical
Interpretation of American History*

*HOW SATAN TURNED AMERICA
AGAINST GOD: A Scriptural Examination
of Conspiracy History*

*GIVEN BY INSPIRATION: A Multifaceted
Study on the A.V. 1611 with
Contemporary Analysis*

*HOLY GROUND: The True History
of the State of Israel*

*PERILOUS TIMES: Deep Truths
for Shallow Waters*

WHAT MUST I DO TO BE SAVED?

William P. Grady, Ph.D.

GRADY
PUBLICATIONS, INC.

ISBN 978-0-9628809-6-4

Library of Congress Control Number: 2024900624

First Printing, March 2024

Scan QR Code for
complimentary audio book
narrated by the author.

For information, address:
GRADY PUBLICATIONS, INC.
P.O. Box 6381
Maryville, TN 37802
Phone: (865) 216-3483

william.grady@gradypublications.com

www.gradypublications.com

Follow us on and @ Grady Publications

About the Cover

THE DRAMATIC COVER was created by Dan Erdmann, a devoted Christian and one of America's leading illustrators. The scene is taken from the sixteenth chapter of Acts (the fifth book of the New Testament, circa AD 50). The Apostle Paul and his co-laborer Silas had been arrested in the Greek city of Philippi (their first missionary stop in Europe), for the "crime" of preaching the Gospel. After the magistrates had them beaten, they were remanded to the jailer for safe keeping, "Who, having received such a charge, thrust them into the inner prison, and made their feet fast in the stocks." (Acts 16:24)

However, as these men were not your average "cussing convicts," at midnight they began praying and singing praises to God (verse 25). Luke records what follows: "And suddenly there was a great earthquake, so that the foundations of the prison were shaken: and immediately all the doors were opened, and every one's bands were loosed" (verse 26). The startled guard, jolted awake by the divine shockwave, "and seeing the prison doors open, he drew out his sword, and would have killed himself, supposing that the prisoners had been fled" (verse 27). As the man was likely a retired veteran Roman soldier, suicide was instinctive, as a security breach on his watch would be a capital offense charge.

But—*Hallelujah*—just in the nick of time, "Paul cried with a loud voice, saying, Do thyself no harm: for we are all here" (verse 28). This turn of events triggered the momentous question: "Then he called for a light, and sprang in, and came trembling, and fell down before Paul and Silas, And brought them out, and said, **Sirs, what must I do to be saved?**" (verses 29-30).

The purpose of this book is to carefully explain Paul's inspired reply—the identical message *you* need to appropriate as well. My prayer is that God will grant you the same humility and wisdom He bestowed upon that anonymous corrections officer some 2,000 years ago.

DANIEL PATRICK GRADY
August 26, 1976 – December 28, 2022

Dedication

THIS BOOK IS lovingly dedicated to the memory of our late son, Daniel Patrick Grady, who departed this life on December 28, 2022, at the young age of forty-six. While his mother and I were devastated at this unexpected event (as were his wife, five children, and two siblings), our collective grief has been supernaturally assuaged by the realization that he knew the Lord Jesus Christ as his personal Saviour, having previously discovered, *and* acted upon the all-important answer to the title question of this volume, "What Must I Do to Be Saved?"

As the Apostle Paul wrote, "We are confident, I say, and willing rather to be absent from the body, and to be present with the Lord," (II Corinthians 5:8), we *know*—beyond any shadow of doubt—that we will see our son again in Heaven. And, because of this truth, we can also appropriate that other exhortation from Paul, "that ye sorrow not, even as others which have no hope." (I Thessalonians 4:13)

The Bible teaches that suffering is designed to produce spiritual power for God's work (Romans 5:3-4). Dr. A. W. Tozer, wrote, "It is doubtful whether God can bless a man greatly until he has hurt him deeply." Thus, as the well-known Scripture, John 3:16, reveals that God Himself had to offer up *His* Son so that sinners could be saved, my wife and I are hopeful that *our* loss might become *your* gain as you examine the following pages. In fact, as a testimony to Jesus, rather than succumb to depression, Linda chose to start her proofreading of this manuscript on the one-year anniversary of Dan's Homegoing.

Finally, our son wrote a song describing his love for the Lord, entitled, "Who You Are." I felt led to include a QR code of him singing this piece in his home church in 2013. Should any be interested in viewing it, keep in mind that the songwriter is *now* doing the very thing he longed for in his lyrics— *"gazing upon the face of God."* (I John 3:2)

Table of Contents

Introduction

What I Already Know About You!

T his book was written for people who love God and want to know for *sure* how they can spend eternity with Him in Heaven! The best way for us to begin our study is for you to learn exactly *how* this timely book "just happened" to fall into your hands; and, more importantly, *why* you are reading it this very moment. The reason behind this propitious development tells me several things about you.

First, while I may not know you personally, I can reasonably conclude that certain recent trials in your life have made you more interested in reaching out to God than usual. The normal shortlist would include family problems, health challenges, and/or financial reversals. Perhaps the escalating global chaos (especially in this country) has gotten your attention. In the celebrated parable of "The Prodigal Son," it was only *after* the young profligate "began to be in want" that "he came to himself" and said, "How many hired servants of my father's have bread enough and to spare, and I perish with hunger! I will arise and **go to my father**." (Luke 15:14, 17-18)

The Holy Bible (King James Version) contains many Scriptures that show how the Lord is always willing to meet an inquiring sinner more than halfway. For instance, Isaiah 44:3 says, "For I will pour water upon him that is thirsty, and floods upon the dry ground." In other words, whenever God knows that a person is searching for spiritual light, He will faithfully honor that desire by revealing himself *to* that individual.

Consider the following additional samples: "Draw nigh to God, **and he will draw nigh to you**" (James 4:8); "The LORD is with you, while ye be with him; **and if ye seek him, he will be found of you**" (II Chronicles 15:2); "Therefore say thou unto them, Thus saith the

LORD of hosts; **Turn ye unto me**, saith the LORD of hosts, **and I will turn unto you**, saith the LORD of hosts" (Zechariah 1:3).

At the dawn of Christianity, a Roman centurion named Cornelius and a business woman named Lydia became two of the earliest converts to the faith. In both cases, the Biblical account shows that the Lord brought the Gospel *to* them only *after* they sought Him out first (see Acts 10:1-6 and 16:13-15). This is nothing to take lightly—the veritable Creator of the universe condescending to help His creation understand His words! King David was overwhelmed with such a reality, declaring, "When I consider thy heavens, the work of thy fingers, the moon and the stars, which thou hast ordained; **What is man, that thou art mindful of him**?" (Psalm 8:3-4)

Second, I am also able to discern that you are undoubtedly a person of strong moral character. At least this would be the opinion of the one who gave you this book. In the "Sermon on the Mount," Jesus said, "Give not that which is holy unto the dogs, **neither cast ye your pearls before swine**." (Matthew 7:6) This means that if a particular sinner has "I hate God" tattooed on his forehead, and is picking his teeth with a switchblade, you might want to find a more favorable prospect for the Lord's precious truths (described here as "pearls").

Solomon gave a similar directive in Proverbs 9:8, "**Reprove not a scorner**, lest he hate thee: rebuke a wise man, and he will love thee." This would further imply that you are also more of a humble person then a prideful person. The former is normally willing to acknowledge when he or she has been wrong about something (in this case, having believed the wrong doctrine for getting to Heaven). James 4:6 says, "God resisteth the **proud**, but giveth grace unto the **humble**." People with character (i.e., the opposite of "swine") are used to doing *right* by *reflex*. Applying that principle to this book, the author's prayerful anticipation is that you would likewise do the right thing now (concerning God's plan of salvation) *if* you only knew what it was.

Consequently, another sign that God has you on His Heavenly radar is that you will find yourself comprehending *and* agreeing with the scriptural flow of *this* book (unlike the many times you "dissed" those pesky Jehovah Witnesses at your door). In John 7:17, Jesus says, "**If any man will do his will**, he shall know of the doctrine, whether it be of God, or whether I speak of myself." A submissive heart attitude to whatever the Lord may desire one to do will ultimately lead to that person's ability to grasp His divine revelation. This is significant, as I Corinthians 2:14 states that *no* one can understand the Scriptures in his or her natural state. The sole exception is when God the Holy Spirit chooses to intervene within that person's human spirit (Luke 24:45). Thus, even David—the man who penned the famous 23rd Psalm—had to pray accordingly, "Open thou **mine** eyes, that I may behold wondrous things out of thy law." (Psalm 119:18)

Furthermore, not only will the Lord help you to comprehend what you will be reading throughout this book, but He will also gently nudge you along with the internal assurance that it is true; and, that consequently you need to act on what it says. Jesus also said, *"No man can come to me, except the Father which hath sent me* **draw him.**" (John 6:44) That one verse will explain why you will continue to experience such a surreal feeling in your soul as you move from truth to truth. The one who told Peter in Matthew 4:19, "Follow me, and I will make you fishers of men," is praying that you will allow the Father to draw *you* into His Gospel net as well.

The final thing I know about you is your potential value to God. The so-called "scarcity principle" states that the rarer an item is, the higher it tends to be valued (e.g., diamonds being costlier than sand). Therefore, should you follow through to the end of this book and embrace the Biblical requirement for salvation, you will have beaten the odds! Jesus said in Matthew 7:13-14, "Enter ye in at the strait gate: for wide is the gate, and broad is the way, that leadeth to destruction, **and many there be which go in thereat**: because strait is the gate, and narrow is the way, which leadeth unto life, **and few there be that find it**." Thus, sadly, only a small percentage of humanity will ever make it to Heaven. He then adds the warning that many religious folks will also land in Hell: "**Many** will say to me in that day, Lord, Lord, have we not prophesied in thy name? and in thy name have cast out devils? and in thy name done many wonderful works? And then will I profess unto them, **I never knew you: depart from me, ye that work iniquity.**" (Matthew 7:22-23)

In closing, the first person of African heritage to embrace Christianity was described in Acts 8:27 as "a man of Ethiopia, an eunuch of great authority under Candace queen of the Ethiopians, who had the charge of all her treasure." A recent proselyte to Judaism, the fellow was returning home from a religious pilgrimage to Jerusalem. Once again, notice how *his* interest in finding the Lord resulted in the Lord "finding" *him*! In verse 28, we see him sitting in his chariot, reading a copy of the Old Testament book of Isaiah. While he is scratching his head as to the meaning of chapter fifty-three (a major prophecy confirming that Jesus Christ was the long-awaited Jewish Messiah), the Holy Spirit directed Philip the evangelist to "Go near, and join thyself to this chariot." Their key exchange follows:

> And Philip ran thither to him, and heard him read the prophet Esaias, and said, Understandest what thou readest? And he said, **How can I, except some man should guide me?** And he desired Philip that he would come up and sit with him. (Acts 8:30-31)

After Philip "preached unto him Jesus," the story concludes beautifully with the eunuch's conversion and baptism in verse 39.

Thus, it is *my* heartfelt desire to be *your* spiritual "guide" as we make our way through the following chapters, examining the pertinent Scriptures together. (As I Corinthians 3:9 says, "For we are laborers together with God," the Gospel of John and Paul's epistle to the Romans have also been included as an appendix for your added edification.) And don't forget—the Bible-believing Christian who gave you this book is no doubt praying for you as well.

> "And ye shall seek me, and find me, when ye
> shall search for me with all your heart."
> (Jeremiah 29:13)

"And Philip ran thither to him, and heard him read the prophet Esaias, and said, Understandest thou what thou readest?

And he said, How can I, except some man should guide me? And he desired Philip that he would come up and sit with him."

(Acts 8:30-31)

1

A Rope of Sand

THE INITIAL PURPOSE of this book is to deprogram the reader from man-made "religion" in order to ground him, or her, on the truth of God's word, as revealed in the Holy Bible. The most important lesson to unlearn is the false notion that Heaven is a *reward* that is earned on earth by doing more good deeds than bad ones (i.e., a works-based salvation).

The classic notion has the departed soul shaking in his boots at the "Pearly Gates" while good ole St. Peter reviews his life (ostensibly to see if he was good *enough* to make it in). When I was a teenager, the lyrics of a popular rock and roll song entitled "Last Kiss" perfectly illustrated this false belief. Grieving over his girlfriend's death from a car wreck, the youthful driver laments:

> Oh, where, oh where can my baby be?
> The Lord took her away from me.
> She's gone to Heaven, **so I got to be good,**
> So I can see my baby when I leave this world.

For a more recent example, in a July 6, 2023, interview with Daniel A. Bonevac, Professor of Philosophy at the University of Texas at Austin, on the subject of religion, Bill O'Reilly stated, "It all comes down to what you want to believe. So, I'm a Roman Catholic, and I want to believe in a just God. And I want to believe that after you die, you're judged on whether you are a good or bad human being by a just and all-knowing God. And that if you're a good human being you're rewarded; if you're not, you suffer. That's what I *want* to believe."

The widespread idea that the way folks live "down *here*" will determine whether (or not) they'll make it "up *there*" constitutes the universal foundation of *every* belief structure on this planet—except, of course, for biblical Christianity. And yet, it is so easy to debunk, even by one's simple God-given logic.

"COME NOW AND LET US REASON TOGETHER"

Isaiah 1:18 says, "Come now, and let us **reason** together, saith the LORD: though your sins be as scarlet, they shall be as white as snow; though they be red like crimson, they shall be as wool." The King James Bible contains a total of 31,102 verses. If I could quote only one Scripture to help guide you to "reason" your way through the utter absurdity that lost sinners can somehow earn their own way into Heaven—it would be the Apostle Paul's inspired words in Galatians 2:21, "I do not frustrate the grace of God: **for if righteousness come by the law, then Christ is dead in vain.**"

The beloved hymn "Amazing Grace" (written in 1799 by the converted slave trader John Newton) has been called the "national anthem of the Christian Church," maintaining a strong appeal among saints and sinners alike (especially at funerals). Unfortunately, however, most religious people have never "reasoned" their way through the basic definition of the word "grace" (despite the fact that they understand what a "grace period" means for their mortgage payments and monthly bills). In the 1828 *American Dictionary of the English Language* by Noah Webster (hereafter called *Webster's 1828 Dictionary*), the word "grace" is defined as "the free **unmerited** love and favor of God."

Paul begins verse 21 with a precursor statement (for the bomb he's going to drop at the end of the text) by declaring that he is not *about* to "frustrate **the grace of God**" ("grace" being the means God uses to get undeserving sinners into Heaven) by endorsing a works-based salvation model. He then proceeds with a purely facetious supposition, "...**for if righteousness comes by the law**...," i.e., should sinners ultimately be judged "righteous" enough to enter Heaven based on how well they kept the "Law of Moses" (otherwise known as the Ten Commandments). He then connects the dots by stating the obvious. *If* such a preposterous idea *was* possible— "...**then Christ is dead in vain.**" In other words, if there was *anything* that a lost person could do for himself—to merit his own salvation—WHY IN THE WORLD WOULD GOD HAVE HAD TO SEND HIS ONLY BEGOTTEN SON TO EARTH TO DIE

ON THE CROSS? Jesus could have stayed in Heaven and simply led a cheerleading squad on our behalf!

This salient verse presents the ultimate bottom line as to why nobody will *ever* get to Heaven based on personal merit. The mother of all mic drops is that the Bible categorically condemns the humanistic notion that a person can be saved by his or her own good works. The following sample will make that abundantly clear:

> "For by **grace** are ye saved through **faith**; and that **not of yourselves**: it is the **gift** of God: **Not of works**, lest any man should boast." (Ephesians 2:8-9)
>
> "...**God; Who hath saved us**, and called us with an holy calling, **not according to our works**, but according to his own purpose and **grace**, which was given us in Christ Jesus before the world began...." (II Timothy 1:8-9)
>
> "**Not by works of righteousness which we have done**, but **according to his mercy he saved us**, by the washing of regeneration, and renewing of the Holy Ghost...." (Titus 3:5)
>
> "Now we know that what things soever the law saith, it saith to them who are under the law: that every mouth may be stopped, and all the world may become guilty before God. **Therefore by the deeds of the law there shall no flesh be justified in his site**: for by the law is the knowledge of sin." (Romans 3:19-20)
>
> "Therefore we conclude that a man is justified by faith **without the deeds of the law**." (Romans 3:28)
>
> "Now to him that worketh is the reward not reckoned of grace, but of debt. **But to him that worketh not**, but believeth on him that justifieth the ungodly, his faith is counted for righteousness." (Romans 4:4-5)
>
> "**And if by grace, then it is no more of works**: otherwise grace is no more grace. But if it be of works, then it is no more grace: otherwise work is no more work." (Romans 11:6)

And so—to return full circle from where we began at Galatians 2:21—note how the Apostle had already thrice reiterated this truth just five verses earlier:

> "Knowing that **a man is not justified by the works of the law, but by the faith of Jesus Christ,** even we have believed in Jesus Christ, that we might be justified by the faith of Christ, **and not by**

the works of the law: for by the works of the law shall no flesh be justified.” (Galatians 2:16)

D. L. MOODY

The colorful evangelist Dwight L. Moody was a household name in late nineteenth-century America. One day he was riding on a train in Utah when the conductor went out of his way to introduce himself to the famous preacher. As a devoted member of The Church of Jesus Christ of Latter-Day Saints (more commonly known as the Mormons), the man made an impassioned effort to convert Mr. Moody to the teachings of Joseph Smith. At the end of their discussion, the Christian revivalist (who would address 100,000,000 people throughout his forty-five-year ministry), summarized their theological impasse accordingly: “There are only two letters’ difference between my religion and yours; you spell yours DO; I spell mine DONE” (i.e., Christ having *done* for us what we could not *do* for ourselves).

GEORGE WHITEFIELD

Finally, one of the most powerful foreign preachers to ever grace this county was an Anglican evangelist by the name of George Whitefield. He made seven trips to nascent America over a century before D. L. Moody. All told, Reverend Whitefield spoke at least 18,000 times to perhaps 10 million listeners in Great Britain and her colonies in the New World. The Holy Spirit bore consistent witness to his labors with thousands of conversions, resulting in a widespread revival known as the Great Awakening.

Mr. Whitefield preached his last outdoor sermon in Exeter, New Hampshire, on September 29, 1770. Having begun his spiritual journey with the moniker “The Boy Preacher with the Golden Voice,” the grizzled veteran would now end the same as “The Grand Itinerant.” Though suffering from severe asthma, Whitefield addressed a throng of over 6,000 spellbound listeners for two solid hours, all the time while balancing himself on a board laid upon a couple of hogsheads.

With less than twenty-four hours to live (he would die early the following morning in the parsonage of the Old South Presbyterian Church in Newburyport, Massachusetts), the faithful man of God ended his thirty-four-year ministry by speaking to the very theme of this chapter. Appropriately enough, he chose his text from II Corinthians 13:5, "Examine yourselves, whether ye be in the faith." The following eyewitness account comes from *The Life of the Rev. George Whitefield,* vol. 2, by Luke Tyerman:

> His voice was hoarse, his enunciation heavy. Sentence after sentence was thrown off in rough, disjointed portions, without much regard for point or beauty. At length, his mind kindled and his lion-like voice roared to the extremities of his audience. He was speaking of the inefficiency of works to merit salvation, and suddenly cried out in a tone of thunder, **Works! works! a man get to heaven by works! I would as soon think of climbing to the moon on a rope of sand!**

2

The Passing Grade

I N THE FALL of 1971, I was employed as a marketing representative for the Brandywine Cash Register Company in Wilmington, Delaware. My biggest sale that year was supplying a cutting-edge, German manufactured electronic bar control system to Bill and Jill Stevenson, co-owners of the "Diamond State's" premier nightclub, the Stone Balloon Tavern and Concert Hall in Newark. (Through the mysterious providence of God, the female partner in the deal would later divorce her husband to marry then-Senator Joe Biden, the forty-sixth president of the United States.)

Because there was so much potential revenue at stake, my boss assigned the sales manager to help me close the deal. I liked working with "Paul M." Besides being a cool guy, he was also the top producer in our firm and I intended to learn all I could from him. However, one day, he asked me a totally out-of-the-blue "religious" question that threw me for a loop. "Bill, if you died today, do you know 100% for sure that you would go to Heaven, or do you have some doubt?"

While the direction of his question would eventually change my life forever, I was initially taken aback for two reasons: I knew that Paul, like me, had grown up in the strictest Roman Catholic tradition, the two of us even graduating from the same prestigious Catholic high school, Salesianum School (the largest parochial institution in Delaware), and "good" Catholics *never* talked that way (bingo, beer, and broads, yes; the Bible? no way, Jose!) And with salvation being determined by our good works (or so I certainly thought at the time), how could anybody know for *sure* that they were going to Heaven? Of course, when I replied that I didn't know what the "blank" he was talking about, he attempted to tell me what the Bible said about the matter, whereupon I shut him down in a New York minute!

The pitiful thing was that after attending Roman Catholic schools for 12 years I had never even *seen* a Catholic "Bible" (much less a King James Version), and consequently was unaware of the Lord's marvelous assurance in I John 5:13, "These things have I written unto you that believe on the name of the Son of God; that ye may **know** that ye have eternal life, and that ye may be believe on the name of the Son of God."

So, what if *you* were asked that same question? What would *your* response be? While most folks will answer, "I *think* so," or "I *hope* so," or "I'm *pretty* sure," etc., the common denominator of all these replies incorporates a cautious optimism, because, once again, the works-based formula of all organized religions must always leave their adherents with some measure of lingering doubt.

But it doesn't stop there. This nagging uncertainty, about so important a matter, produces an inescapable paranoia—i.e., what comes after death? (Just observe how the average person fidgets at a funeral.) Thus, the Bible says that one of the main reasons Jesus went to the Cross was to set men free from this universal trepidation. "But we see Jesus, who was made a little lower than the angels for the suffering of death, crowned with glory and honour; that he by the grace of God should taste death for every man...**And deliver them who through fear of death were all their lifetime subject to bondage**." (Hebrews 2:9,15)

Now the great key to gaining this victory is discovering the most important fact that organized religion conveniently fails to mention. While everyone is told that they must do more good deeds than bad ones for God to accept them into Heaven, the desperate sinner is never told just *how* good he or she has to be. For instance, when I attended Salesianum, the passing grade for any subject was 70%. (Today, it is generally 60%.) Because flunking God's test for Heaven or Hell is obviously more critical than bombing a mere high school exam, why don't *we* know how high the theoretical "salvation bar" is set?

Well, suppose I told you that not even a 99% score would be good enough to get you through those pearly gates? You say, "Preacher, that's preposterous!" From a human standpoint, I would agree; but don't miss God's caution light in Proverbs 14:12, "There is a way which seemeth right unto a man, but the end thereof are the ways of death:" The purpose of this book is for you to discover the Lord's answer to that eternal question: *"What must I do to be saved?"* The Bible makes it abundantly clear that should any person opt to place his or her faith for getting into Heaven in their own track record on earth, they will need a passing grade of 100%! Note how Paul states this critical truth *twice* in that same epistle to the churches of Galatia:

"For as many as are of the works of the law are under the curse: for it is written, Cursed is every one that continueth not in **all things** which are written in the book of the law to do them." (Galatians 3:10)

"For I testify again to every man that is circumcised, that he is a debtor to do **the whole law**." (Galatians 5:3)

The Holy Spirit then has James supply the knockout punch that settles the issue once and for all—that God demands absolute perfection (while knowing that no one can measure up accordingly).

"For whosoever shall keep the whole law, and yet offend in one point, he is guilty of all." (James 2:10)

This totally *unattainable* standard is one of the very first lessons that appears in the Holy Bible. After the Lord confronts Adam (and his wife) for committing only one "itsy-bitsy, teenie weenie" sin (partaking of the forbidden fruit), Genesis 3:24 tells us, "So he drove **out** the man...."

The greatest Bible illustration that the Ten Commandments can't save anyone—due to this 100% "passing grade" —was provided by none other than the great "Lawgiver of Israel" himself! After Moses delivered the Jews from Egypt, he faithfully led them through the wilderness for forty long years. However, when the time came for the nation to enter Canaan, God refused to let Moses in, assigning Joshua to take the helm.

To make a long story short, the main reason why this occurred was because Moses had also committed what appeared to be just one "small" isolated sin. When the people ran out of water, God told Moses to strike a rock with his rod and the water would flow out (Exodus 17:6). He was then instructed that from thenceforth he would merely have to *speak* to the rock to get additional water (Numbers 20:8). However, because the Jews were driving him crazier than normal, "Mo" lost his temper and *smote* the rock—*again*—rather than merely speaking to it (Numbers 20:11).

Without getting too deep in the New Testament, Paul enlightens us that this "rock" was actually a picture (or type) of Jesus Christ (I Corinthians 10:4). The "smiting" of the rock was a further type of Jesus dying for our sins on the Cross (Isaiah 53:4). The key doctrinal truth here is that Jesus only had to die ONCE for our sins. Thus, for Moses to have struck the rock more than one time destroyed this teaching. This is precisely what the Roman Catholic "Church" does on a weekly basis with their blasphemous lie that Jesus is "re-sacrificed" in the Mass every Sunday. (See Hebrews 9:26-28; 10:2, 10-14.)

And so, for making this *one* serious "error," the human vessel who literally gave us the Ten Commandments, was ultimately denied the privilege of entering the "Promised Land" itself. His parting words to the Jews were full of pathos:

"Furthermore the LORD was angry with me for your sakes, and sware that I should not go over Jordan, and that I should not go in unto that good land, which the LORD thy God giveth thee for an inheritance: But I must die in this land, I must not go over Jordan: but ye shall go over, and possess that good land." (Deuteronomy 4:21-22)

This dramatic development was God's way of magnifying the scary truth of James 2:10, "For whosoever shall keep the whole law, **and yet offend in one point**, he is guilty of **all**." But *Hallelujah*, the story doesn't end there! While Moses, the Bible's main type of the Law, could not get the people into Canaan because of *one* infraction, Joshua, a major Bible type of Jesus, could and did! The Old Testament name "Joshua" literally means "Jehovah saves" (while Acts 7:45 and Hebrews 4:8 reveal how "Jesus" is the New Testament equivalent of "Joshua.")

Finally, this great doctrinal truth—that *sinful* men require a *sinless* Saviour because they cannot measure up to the Lord's perfect standard—was summarized by the Apostle Paul in two simple words: "For all have sinned, and **come short** of the glory of God." (Romans 3:23) While any person can feel "pretty good" about their perceived virtue when compared to other sinners, everything changes when we contrast our righteousness with the righteousness of Jesus Christ. "But we are all as an unclean thing, **and all our righteousnesses are as filthy rags**; and we all do fade as a leaf; and our iniquities, like the wind, have taken us away." (Isaiah 64:6)

In 1775, Rev. Augustus M. Toplady, a minister in the Church of England, wrote the beloved hymn, "Rock of Ages." Second only to "Amazing Grace" in its enduring popularity, Toplady's second stanza highlights the utter inability of sinful man to make God's passing grade:

> Not the labors of my hands
> Can fulfill Thy law's demands;
> Could my zeal no respite know,
> Could my tears forever flow,
> All for sin could not atone;
> Thou must save, and Thou alone.

3

The Divine Dilemma

THE BIBLE SAYS in Job 22:21, "Acquaint now thyself with him, and be at peace: thereby good shall come unto thee." One of the great keys to discovering and understanding God's plan of salvation is to "acquaint thyself" with the holy fact that your Creator has *two* distinct natures that function simultaneously. Though both of these divine characters are revealed in Scripture, man-made "religion" has consistently emphasized one to the total exclusion of the other.

The first of these dual natures is His love. The Apostle John (who also happens to be called "that disciple whom Jesus loved" in John 21:7) penned the definitive text on this subject, "Beloved, let us love one another: for love is of God; and every one that loveth is born of God, and knoweth God. He that loveth not knoweth not God; **for God is love**." (I John 4:7-8)

A sacred Christian hymn that extols the Lord's ineffable heart was published in 1919 under the title, "The Love of God." The author was a German-American Nazarene songwriter by the name of Frederick M. Lehman. Having heard a powerful sermon on God's love in a camp meeting, the following day the bi-vocational pastor found himself meditating on the message while doing manual labor (packing oranges and lemons in containers) in a California factory. Overwhelmed with inspiration, Lehman scrambled during a break to pen the first two stanzas (and the refrain) of his now famous song—on crates and scraps of paper.

> The love of God is greater far
> Than tongue or pen can ever tell;
> It goes beyond the highest star,
> And reaches to the lowest hell;
> The guilty pair, bowed down with care,

God gave His Son to win;
His erring child He reconciled,
And pardoned from his sin.

Refrain:
Oh, love of God, how rich and pure!
How measureless and strong!
It shall forevermore endure—
The saints' and angels' song.

When hoary time shall pass away,
And earthly thrones and kingdoms fall,
When men who here refuse to pray,
On rocks and hills and mountains call,
God's love so sure, shall still endure,
All measureless and strong;
Redeeming grace to Adam's race—
The saints' and angels' song.

For his third and final stanza, Lehman recalled having heard another preacher quote a poem in his message that seemed to fit the melody and meter perfectly. According to tradition, the piece was found scratched on a cell wall by a prisoner some two centuries ago. It is not known for sure whether the words were original or if the man had heard them previously and inscribed them for his personal comfort. (One legend even attributes the verse to an eleventh-century rabbi, written in Hebrew.)

After the inmate died, a work crew was assigned to repaint his cell. When the men discovered the words, they were deeply moved. Thanks to divine providence, rather than brush them away to obscurity, one of the workers jotted down the poem for posterity. (Note the ironic parallel with the "Love of God" stretched across the "parchment" of a prison wall.)

Could we with ink the ocean fill
And were the skies of parchment made
Were every stalk on earth a quill.
And every man a scribe by trade;
To write the love of God above
Would drain the ocean dry;
Nor could the scroll contain the whole;
Though stretched from sky to sky.

While I John 4:8 identifies the personification of "love" as God Almighty Himself, John 3:16 represents the verse most commonly associated with the subject as it reveals the greatest illustration of love in action. "For God **so loved** the world, **that he gave** his only begotten Son, that whosoever believeth in him should not perish, but have everlasting life."

Here, the Father is basically saying that He would rather have Jesus *die* than to have *you* go to Hell! And, if that's where you wind up, you would have landed there over His Son's (temporarily) dead body! True love always gives. Conversely, as Romans 5:8 states that God proved His love by *giving* us His Son, those who have accepted that gift are to show *their* love *to* God by giving Him *their* unfeigned obedience: Thus, Jesus said in John 14:15, "**If** ye love me, **keep** my commandments."

The popular sports personality Tim Tebow has long understood this holy principle. While Tim's parents were serving as Baptist missionaries in the Philippines, his mother, Pam, was strongly advised to get an abortion due to life-threatening complications. She refused and turned her unborn son's destiny over to the Lord. The rest is history. In the 2009 BCS National Championship game between Florida and Oklahoma, the grateful Heisman Trophy winner wrote "John 3:16" in eye black under his eyes. During the contest, over 90 million people Googled the verse, making it the number one topic trending on Facebook and Twitter! (For the record, this did *not* occur when the pagan professional wrestler, Steve "Stone Cold" Austin, mockingly promoted the moniker "Austin 3:16.")

Exactly three years later, Tebow inadvertently did it again during his first NFL playoff game with the Denver Broncos against the Pittsburgh Steelers (which he won in overtime thanks to a game winning 80-yard touchdown pass). In what has come to be known as the "Mile High Miracle," Tim reportedly passed for 316 yards and averaged 31.6 yards per pass and 3.16 yards per carry. The final quarter-hour television rating for that game was 31.6. Ben Roethlisberger, quarterback for the Steelers, threw a pass on 3rd and 16 that was intercepted and Pittsburg's time of possession was an incredible 31 minutes and 6 seconds! (Someone has rightly said that "a coincidence is God's way of remaining anonymous.")

JUDEX DAMATUR CUM NOCENS ABSOLVITUR

However, there's a critical buzzword contained in John 3:16 that cracks the door open to that *other* nature of God—the "Debbie Downer" one that most folks don't want to hear about; it's that pesky little word "perish." Here, we are apparently confronted by the spiritual conundrum of a *loving* God who can coexist with a *perishing* human. What's *that* all about? (Those smiling, money-grabbing, Hell-bound televangelists, like Joel Osteen, are not *about* to touch this one with a ten-foot pole.)

The answer to this dilemma has to do with His lesser-known nature. At least three Bible words can be used to identify this suppressed part of the Lord's character. They are His *holiness*; *justice*; and *wrath*. Thus, an antithetical appearing verse to I John 4:8, *"for God is **love**,"* would be Hebrews 12:29, *"For our God is a **consuming fire**."* Considered in their proper order, the best explanation for this threefold description of God's so-called "darker" side is that, because the Lord is *holy*, He must exercise *justice*, and this process will inevitably evoke *wrath* upon the guilty. The genesis of His wrath falling on the human race began with our first parents in the Garden of Eden (i.e., the "guilty pair, bowed down with care," referenced in Lehman's first stanza). At this point it might behoove you to remember exactly what makes a person guilty: *"For whosoever shall keep the whole law, and yet offended in **one** point, he is **guilty of all**."* (James 2:10)

Another example of the typical sinner's selective hearing loss is the previously mentioned iconic hymn, "Amazing Grace." My, how people *love* to hear this song, especially on bagpipes! That first stanza is absolutely mesmerizing:

> Amazing grace! how sweet the sound,
> That saved a wretch like me!
> I once was lost, but now am found,
> Was blind, but now I see.

And the same kudos go out for stanzas three and four. However, it's that second stanza that the religious crowd avoids like the plague:

> 'Twas grace that taught my heart to **fear**,
> And grace my **fears** relieved;
> How precious did that grace appear
> The hour I first believed.

The consternation here (similar to that word *perish* in John 3:16) goes something like this: *If* "God is love" (and He certainly is), what would we possibly have to fear? After all, didn't former President Franklin Delano Roosevelt say, "The only thing we have to fear is fear itself?"

The bottom line to the *holiness, justice,* and *wrath* sequence is that God cannot possibly allow sin—*any* sin, even *one*—to go unpunished. And just to help you know how the Bible defines "sin," I John 3:4 says, "Whosoever committeth sin transgressesth also the law: **for sin is the transgression of the law.**" (Furthermore, as James 4:17 reveals, God also delineates sins of *omission*; "Therefore to him that knoweth to do good, and doeth it not, to him it is sin.")

Talk about a scary reality; were the Lord to allow even *one* transgression to go unpunished, *the entire universe would implode* because God would then cease to be God! An ancient legal proverb (attributed to the first-century Latin writer Publilus Syrus) encapsulates this concept with the phrase: *judex damnatur cum nocens absolvitur.* Translation in formal equivalence: "The judge is condemned when the guilty is acquitted."

Not only must we "acquaint ourselves with Him" regarding the unnerving fact of His "*dual* natures," but secondly, with the related fact of His "*dueling* natures," or what I call "The Divine Dilemma." A black preacher once delivered a sermon entitled, "Did it ever occur to you that nothing occurs to God?" While the Lord certainly knew in eternity past that Adam and Eve would plunge the human race into sin, He also permitted this act to place Him in a quandary of sorts (i.e., as seen from *our* flawed perspective). The following illustration will reveal this "Divine Dilemma."

In the mind of God, the human race was originally designed to spend eternity with Him. And so, after the fall in Eden (with its subsequent penalty of death), whenever you were to die, God would instinctively want to pull you into Heaven to be with Him. However, because sin has now entered the world, a "slight" problem exists. Right before God's *love* would set you on that street of pure gold, His other nature would kick in, automatically spinning you around to head for that "*other* place."

But now, watch *this*! Just before you would be plunged into Hell (because of God's *holiness, justice,* and *wrath*), His *love* nature would automatically kick in. This side of God would be aghast at the prospect of you burning in Hell, primarily because you would not be fellowshipping with Him for eternity. So, back toward Heaven you would bounce, only to be barred once again by—you got it—His *holiness, justice*, and *wrath*.

Of course, this illustrative ping-pong cycle could not continue indefinitely. Sooner or later, sinners would have to wind up in one place or the other. Thus, the question begs—Which of these dual natures is the stronger? (Hint: Just drop anything out of your hand and see which direction it goes.) If you are driving your car and your feet press the accelerator and the brake at the same time, the break will override the gas pedal every time. Make no mistake about it neighbor; God's *holiness* will likewise take precedence over His *love* every time!!! While David addressed his God in Psalm 89:14 with the words, "mercy and truth shall go before thy face," he prefaced that statement with the qualifier, "Justice and judgment are the *habitation* of thy throne." (*Webster's 1828 Dictionary* defines habitation as: "Place of abode; a *settled* dwelling.")

Therefore, it was imperative for God to devise a plan that would kill two birds with one stone. He had to "find" a way to get *you* into Heaven, to satisfy His *love*—yet without jeopardizing His *holiness* (i.e., by closing His eyes while some angel snuck you in through the back door). In other words, to satisfy *both* natures, He needed a way to get you into Heaven without allowing your sins to go unpunished. Otherwise, He would violate the doctrine of *judex damnatur cum nocens absolvitur*!

"He is the Rock, his work is perfect: for all his ways are judgment:
a God of truth and without iniquity, just and right is he."
(Deuteronomy 32:4)

4

Spiritual Death Row

I KNOW A godly preacher (and wife) in a Southern state who carry a particularly heavy burden. While some Christians have seen their children sent to prison for various crimes, this aged couple has a saved son who has been sitting on death row for decades! I cannot imagine how difficult this "Sword of Damocles" must be for them.

Well, according to Scripture, for you to gain the answer to that eternal question, "What must I do to be saved?" it is essential for you to discover the shocking reality that you too are sitting on death row, only in a spiritual sense. You see—unlike those religious charlatans who abandon you in a fog of doubt about you're never being able to know if you are making that elusive "passing grade" (i.e., that unknown percentage of being more good than bad) —the King James Bible will give it to you straight down the middle, waist high, over the plate!

When babies enter the world, they do so with a fallen nature they inherited from their parents (Genesis 5:3; Romans 5:12). Cute as they may appear, Psalm 58:3 declares, "The wicked are estranged from the womb: they go astray as soon as they be born, **speaking lies.**" (Any mother can attest to how they have rushed to change their screaming tots' diapers only to find them dry as the Sahara Desert.)

However, as Deuteronomy 1:39 shows, because these little ones lack any "knowledge between good and evil," they cannot be held accountable for their sins. Therefore, our merciful Lord grants them a *temporary* "grace period." (Infants born with incurable mental disabilities would come under this same umbrella.) Thus, when King David learned that his baby son had died, he said, "**I shall go to him**, but he shall not return to me." (II Samuel 12:23)

But all this changes when children reach the so-called age of accountability. The moment this occurs (which obviously differs from person-to-person), that boy or girl unknowingly enters *God's* Death Row, the cell door clanging ominously behind. You say, "Dr. Grady, what in *the* world are you talking about?" Well, do you recall the Lord's exhortation to "reason" with Him in Isaiah 1:18? Could you find a more "reasonable" premise than the following statement? The most important prerequisite for getting "saved" is to realize that you are "lost," i.e., that you *need* to be saved in the first place! ("'Twas grace that taught my heart to *fear*," etc.)

A swimmer doesn't call out to the lifeguard unless he or she is convinced that they are drowning. It's the same with being rescued spiritually. You *must* believe that you are going under (i.e., all the way down to Hell). This was Peter's experience when he attempted to walk out on the water to Jesus, "But when he saw the wind boisterous, he was afraid; **and beginning to sink, he cried**, saying, Lord, **save me**." (Matthew 14:30)

The hard facts about *you* being on the Lord's Death Row are simple: Paul wrote in Romans 3:10, "As it is written, there is **none** righteous, no, not one." He then followed up with the text we have previously examined, "For **all** have sinned, and **come short** of the glory of God." (Romans 3:23) But the clincher is the first half of Romans 6:23—"For the wages of sin is **death**...." The Bible affirms that the paycheck we have earned for our sin is death!

Naturally, all rational people understand Benjamin Franklin's famous idiom, "In this world nothing can be said to be certain, except death and taxes." However, they normally acquaint this only with physical death. But, there's also a *spiritual* death to experience for our sins. Hebrews 9:27 says, "And as it is appointed unto men once to die, **but after this the judgment**." (Sadly, while the previously cited Anglican evangelist George Whitefield routinely pressed Franklin about his need to receive Jesus Christ as Saviour, the recalcitrant secularist famously said after Whitefield's passing, "He used, indeed, sometimes to pray for my conversion, but never had the satisfaction of believing his prayers were heard.")

Now as this spiritual "paycheck" can only be issued after we expire, Scripture calls it the "*second* death." Note how John "the beloved" confirmed this gruesome reality in Revelation 21:8, "...all liars, shall have their part in the lake which burneth with fire and brimstone: which is the **second death**." (And remember, just as one murder would make you a murderer, one lie would make you a liar.) This is why you were thrust into God's Death Row the moment you were able to discern right from wrong. You already had your sin nature, passed down from your parents. Now you have to "pay the piper" for your sin—*physical* death in this life; *spiritual* death in the next.

I chose the analogy of a "death row" experience because it is restricted to prisoners who have already had their trial and been sentenced. It is simply the designated status whereupon an inmate awaits his or her execution date. Thus, notice John's use of the present tense (including the Anglo-Saxon suffix): "He that believe**th** on him is not condemned: but he that believe**th** not is **condemned already**, because he hath not believed in the name of the only begotten Son of God." (John 3:18) Another proof text for your current state of condemnation is John 3:36. "He that believe**th** on the Son **hath** everlasting life: and he that believe**th** not the Son shall not see life; but the wrath of God abide**th** on him." (John 3:36)

Yet another example is I John 5:12: "He that **hath** the Son **hath** life; and he that **hath not** the Son of God **hath** not life." (For what it's worth, while sinners try to hide behind the excuse that the King James text is "too archaic to comprehend," note how the entire world will one day be judged by those eighteen *one* syllable words.)

The main difference between man's death row and God's Death Row is that there will never be any stays of execution or any eleventh-hour call from any governor regarding the latter. Your execution date (i.e., the day the "Grim Reaper" comes for you) is set and it's not about to be continued (momentarily or indefinitely). Unlike the world, God's justice is sure. "Because sentence against an evil work is not executed speedily, therefore the heart of the sons of men is fully set in them to do evil." (Ecclesiastes 8:11) Translation: when it's your time to go—you're *gone!*

PULL UP...PULL UP...PULL UP!!

The late Oliver B. Green (1915-1976) was an old-time, Hell-fire and brimstone, Bible-belt evangelist who hailed from Greenville, South Carolina. Besides conducting numerous tent meetings and revivals, the converted bootlegger also maintained an effective radio and printing ministry. One of his more sensational pieces of literature was a 32-page booklet that read, in bright, bold red letters: *What You Have To Do To Go To Hell!* Whenever a curious prospect would open the pamphlet, they would be shocked to discover—nothing—but blank pages!

If you are tempted to doubt what I am saying, simply take this book in your hand; stretch out your arm; and then release it from your grasp. Which way did it go? The greatest physical proof that you need to be saved is the law of *gravity.* Every human being has a downward density by nature. The main reason for this is because the Bible strongly implies that Hell is located in the center of the earth. "Yet thou shalt be brought down to hell, to the sides of the pit." (Isaiah 14:15).

The summary truth here is that you entered this world in a descending trajectory, headed straight for Hell, like a World War II Japanese kamikaze pilot! And unless you pull up on the Gospel throttle—by getting the answer right to our question, "What Must I Do to Be Saved?" —you will make *your* splash landing, not in the Pacific Ocean, but in the Lake of Fire! So, *"Pull up...Pull up...Pull up!!"*

5

Just and the Justifier

YOU ARE NOW about to learn a pivotal truth. So far, we've discovered from the Holy Bible that our perceived good works (or personal merit) could *never* enable us to be admitted into Heaven, solely because the Lord's standard of perfection is totally unattainable. We also learned that when push comes to shove, God's character traits of holiness, justice, and wrath will overrule His love every time. Therefore, our present condition is one of abject condemnation, sitting in spiritual lockup on God's Death Row, awaiting our future execution—which is dropping into a world of hurt, forever (Psalm 9:17 confirming, "The wicked shall be turned into hell....")

And if all this wasn't bad enough, it was also noted that, unlike the death rows in America's penal system, there can be no last-minute stays of execution in our spiritual experience. However—that is *not* to say that all hope is necessarily lost. In fact, it just so happens that there *is* one possible way out of your dilemma. A famous historical novel published in 1859 by Charles Dickens (later made into a feature-length film) utilizes this plot (i.e., *your* potential exit strategy) as the grand finale of the story.

A TALE OF TWO CITIES

"It was the best of times; it was the worst of times," Dickens writes in the opening line of his classic work, *A Tale of Two Cities*. Rather than get bogged down in the complex plot of this popular, though lengthy, narrative, I will confine my synopsis to a thumbnail sketch in order to concentrate on the all-important insightful denouement.

To make a long story short, the year is late 1775 and the dual cities in question are Paris and London. The novel opens with the story of a French physician, Alexandre Manette, his eighteen-year-long imprisonment in the Bastille, and his subsequent release to live in London with his daughter Lucie, whom he has never met. Dickens' two leading characters are Charles Darnay, a French aristocrat and the shrewd British barrister, Sydney Carton. While both men make a play for the charming Mademoiselle Manette, Darnay eventually emerges as the successful suitor, winning Lucie's hand in marriage. Meanwhile, Carton is portrayed as a brilliant but depressed and cynical alcoholic, remorseful for what he views as a wasted life. The unrequited love he feels for Lucie is only exacerbated by her mother-like efforts to inspire him to be a better person.

Fast-forward to 1789 when the Revolution erupts on July 14 with the storming of the Bastille. Amidst the ensuing chaos of the ten-month "Reign of Terror," Darnay is arrested for treason and arraigned before a tribunal on trumped-up charges by one, Madame Defarge. Promptly sentenced to be guillotined the next afternoon, Darnay bravely embraces his fate.

When Carton learns of Darnay's dire situation, he springs into action, determined to save the day for his old friend (not to mention Lucie's impending widowhood). He promptly enlists the aid of a prison spy named John Barsad to help him slip into the facility where the revolutionaries are holding Darnay. Shortly after entering the startled man's cell, Carton drugs Darnay, then quickly changes clothes with him. The disguised prisoner is then removed from the jail—*in his place*. The ruse is successful. No one questions either man's identity as their physical features are nearly identical.

Once outside, Barsad places Darnay into a waiting carriage where Lucie and her family were expecting Carton to return. They then flee to England while Darnay gradually regains consciousness. As the escapees make their way to freedom, the closing scene shifts to their courageous benefactor, who is peering into the future as he contemplates his own departure—from this life—via the guillotine (aka the "National Razor"). His only stated source of solace centers on "the lives for which I lay down my life—peaceful, useful, prosperous and happy, in that England which I shall see no more." He is especially moved at the thought that Darnay and Lucie had named their child after him. He then exclaims with great pathos:

I see that I hold a sanctuary in their hearts, and in the hearts of their descendants, generations hence. I see her, an old woman, weeping for me on the anniversary of this day. I see her and her husband, their course done, lying side by side in their last earthly bed, and I know that each was not more honoured and held sacred in the other's soul, than I was in the souls of both.

As a heavy-duty cotton rope slowly raises the weighted and angled steel blade up its 89-inch wooden frame (adjacent the gruesome, blood-soaked leather basket), "Number 23" utters one of the most celebrated lines in all of literature— "It is a far, far better thing that I do, than I have ever done; it is a far, far, better rest that I go to than I have ever known."

YOU, TOO, HAVE A VISITOR!

While the personal spiritual beliefs of Charles Dickens may have been shrouded in mystery, *A Tale of Two Cities* contains a more surprising ending still. Like the jaw-dropping scene written by that other "Charles" (Shultz) in his 1965 seasonal classic, "A Charlie Brown Christmas," when Linus famously recites Luke 2:8-14 from a King James Bible, Carton's final musing was the apropos assertion by Jesus Christ in John 11:25, "I am the resurrection, and the life: **he that believeth in me**, though he were dead, yet shall he live." (This powerful text conspicuously appears several times through the film and constitutes the concluding visual message displayed across the silver screen.)

Those five little words, "he that believeth in me," have *everything* to do with the answer to our eternity-altering question, "What must I do to be saved?" It also represents the transition from the dramatic closing scene of Carton's fictional place swapping with Darnay and the powerful Bible truth that it illustrates in reality!

As we have already established, every human being in history has landed on God's Death Row when they reached the age of accountability. Once again, no matter how much the Lord may *love* the human race, His *justice* cannot allow their sins to go unpunished. But, herein lies the surprising catch! While the Bible categorically declares that God's judgment on sin is *death*—notice that it doesn't specify exactly *who* has to die. For instance, during the American Civil War, while most Northern men were eligible for Lincoln's draft, the wealthy could avoid conscription by hiring a substitute to serve in their place (one who was otherwise exempt from service).

Now apply this to the spiritual realm. What if a condemned sinner could get someone to take his or her place (i.e., to be punished in *their* stead). Wouldn't that satisfy God's justice? Well, yes and no; yes—but only in a *theoretical* way. That proxy would have to be sinless, right? After all, one condemned prisoner cannot take the place of a fellow condemned inmate, as they're both in the same dire strait.

Consequently, the sinner's *only* hope would be to find a *sinless* fellow human, one who'd be *willing* to make the exchange. Of course, "good luck" on that one, as Romans 3:23 has already declared, "For **all have sinned** and come short of the glory of God." But wait—I hear an angelic corrections officer coming toward your cell with a message, "Prisoner # (your name), you have a visitor."

You say, "Dr. Grady, who could *that* possibly be?" Why—only the *perfect* answer to your question, *"What must I do to be saved?"* More specifically, the one who asked his detractors, *"Which of you **convinceth me of sin**?"* (John 8:46); the one of whom Paul wrote, "For he hath made him to be sin for us, who **knew no sin**" (II Corinthians 5:21); the one of whom the author of Hebrews wrote, "but was in all points tempted like as we are, **yet without sin**" (Hebrews 4:15); the one of whom Peter wrote, "Who did **no sin**" (I Peter 2:22); the one of whom John wrote, "...he was manifested to take away our sins; and in him is **no sin**" (I John 3:5); and finally—the one of whom Pontius Pilate declared— "I find **no fault** in this man" (Luke 23:4).

As I said in the previous chapter, God had to find a way to kill two birds with one stone; He had to somehow get you into Heaven—*without* turning a blind eye to your sins. The divine solution to this problem was three-fold: First, the Father sent His only begotten Son to earth to take on human flesh (John 1:14). Next, your would-be substitute went on to live a perfect, sinless life—the only "man" to do so in history. Last, He voluntarily went to the Cross to pay the penalty for every sin that would ever be committed in history (I John 2:1).

The greatest Bible illustration of this substitutionary (vicarious) atonement (cited in all four gospels) was when the bloodthirsty Jewish mob chose Barabbas—over Jesus Christ—to be released by Pontius Pilate in a customary annual pardon before the feast of Passover. When

Barabbas looked at Calvary as he fled the city his thoughts must have been, "He took *my* place…Jesus is dying on the Cross that *I* deserved."

Which brings this narrative back to you. Even now, Jesus Christ is standing outside *your* death row lockup, willing to take *your* place! However, unlike *A Tale of Two Cities,* you will not be drugged and forcibly removed. You must invite Him in of your own free will. If you agree to do so, He will enter your cell and you will then be free to exit the same. This is the solution to God's dilemma. The Father's *love* can now be satisfied, *without* compromising His *holiness,* for the sin debt *will* be covered. The song writer Gordon Jensen translated this beautiful doctrine to a hymn entitled, "I Should Have Been Crucified."

I was guilty with nothing to say,
And they were coming to take me away,
But then a voice from Heaven was heard that said,
"Let him go, take Me instead."

CHORUS:
And I should have been crucified!
I should have suffered and died!
I should have hung on the cross in disgrace,
But Jesus, God's Son, took my place!

The crown of thorns, the spear in His side,
And all the pain should have been mine.
The rusty nails were meant for me,
But Jesus took them and let me go free.

In closing, the most succinct text that summarizes this marvelous truth is found in Paul's epistle to the church in Rome (i.e., the *real* church):

"Being justified freely by his grace through the redemption that is in Christ Jesus: Whom God hath set forth to be a propitiation through faith in his blood, to declare his righteousness for the remission of sins that are past, through the forbearance of God; To declare, I say, at this time his righteousness: **that he might be just, and the justifier of him which believeth in Jesus**." (Romans 3:24-26)

As James 2:13 puts it, the substitutionary death of Jesus Christ allowed the Father's heart to triumph over His wrath, "…mercy rejoiceth over judgment." In light of this victory, the Psalmist declares, "Mercy and truth are met together; righteousness and peace have kissed each other" (Psalm 85:10). Praise the Lord—that *brake* of God's holiness will no longer stop you at the gates of pearl. You may now put the *pedal* to the *metal* and drive right up that street of gold to your Heavenly mansion (John 14:2).

"Greater love hath no man than this,
that a man lay down his life for his friends."
(John 15:13)

6

The Other Place

THE BIBLE DECLARES in Proverbs 9:10, "The **fear** of the LORD is the beginning of wisdom." More to the point, Hebrews 10:31 warns, "It is a **fearful** thing to fall into the hands of the living God." The secular Jewish-American playwright and screenwriter Rod Serling attempted to scratch the surface of this spiritual truth in the twenty-eighth episode of his award-winning anthology television series, *The Twilight Zone*.

In "A Nice Place to Visit" (broadcast in 1960), career criminal Henry Francis "Rocky" Valentine dies in a police shootout and awakens in what soon *appears* to be the perfect environment. At the direction of his "angelic" guide, one "Mr. Pip" (played by Sebastian Cabot), Rocky begins to experience every conceivable perk (from a small time hoodlum's perspective, that is): a luxurious pad; classy wheels; plenty of gorgeous women ("dolls" as he calls them); winning at every game of "chance" in the casinos; an endless supply of cash; plus, Pip's standing assurance that he can "knock off any bank he prefers," especially as the only "copper" he encounters is a midget.

However, as the inevitable boredom and exasperation sets in (from having his every whim satisfied, while predictably losing at nothing), Rocky pours out his frustration to "Fats" (his affectionate nickname for Pip). "If I gotta stay here another day, I'm gonna go nuts. Look, I don't belong in Heaven, see? I want to go to the *other* place." The episode ends with Mr. Pip's chilling reply, "Heaven? Whatever gave you the idea you were in Heaven, Mr. Valentine? *This **is** the other place!*" As the realization dawns on Rocky's face, he frantically tries to open the now-locked door. "Fats" roars at his desperation, while the camera pans up.

WHAT YOU NEED TO BE SAVED FROM

The twisted takeaway here is simple. The best motivation for *you* to continue *your* pursuit of the Bible's true way to Heaven is to discover what the alternative destination is—the so-called "Other Place." When Jesus described the passing of a certain unsaved Jew in Luke 16:23, He did not mince any words. "The rich man also died and was buried; **And in hell he lift up his eyes, being in torments**...." And just for the record, given the Lord's immutable prerequisite in John 3:3, "...**Except a man be born again, he cannot see the kingdom of God**," the same reality would apply to Rod Serling and Sebastian Cabot (i.e., both men finding *themselves* in the real "other place") if *they* expired without trusting Jesus Christ as *their* personal Saviour!

To revisit Mr. Dickens's tale—with the combined weight of the blade and the mouton (a metal weight), the guillotine can sever a human neck in 0.005 seconds, thus making the ghastly invention one of the most "merciful" methods of execution in the annals of capital punishment. (Sydney Carton's fictional experience was prefigured in Proverbs 12:10, "...the tender mercies of the wicked are cruel.") Conversely, Reverend Charles H. Spurgeon, the celebrated nineteenth-century Baptist pastor in London, once remarked, "The hell of hells will be the thought that it is *forever*."

Yet, according to the Bible itself, Hell does *not* last forever, at least not in a technical sense. While the unconverted *do* go there immediately upon their death, at the future Great White Throne Judgment (described in Revelation 20:11-15) they are summoned up to stand before Jesus Christ to have their life evaluated, not for the possibility of any parole, but rather to determine *how* severe their eternal punishment will be—in a second, permanent location called the "Lake of Fire." (According to Luke 12:47-48, this range of suffering appears to be likened to one being scourged with "*many* stripes" as opposed to "*few* stripes.") In any case, the ghastly final scene is forecast in Revelation 20:15, "And whosoever was not found written in the book of life was **cast into the lake of fire**." Thus, Hell for a time, followed by the Lake of Fire for eternity.

The main common denominators for both abodes are surreal to say the least, and—a *whole* lot worse than "Rocky" Valentine's fictional Hell. Foremost on the list would be the unfathomable experience of *burning forever in unquenchable fire*. When the rich man was able to see Lazarus and Abraham across a great chasm in Paradise (a temporary Old Testament arrangement before the death of Christ), he cried out in vain, "Father Abraham, have mercy on me, and send Lazarus, that he may dip the tip of his finger in water, and cool my tongue; **for I am tormented in this flame**." (Luke 16:24)

Among other references, Jesus said in Matthew 5:22, "...but whosoever shall say, Thou fool, shall be in danger of hell **fire**." According to Matthew 13:50, the holy angels shall take the wicked and "cast them into the **furnace of fire**: [where] there shall be wailing and gnashing of teeth." Matthew 25:41 previews Jesus as telling the condemned, "Depart from me, ye cursed, into **everlasting fire**...." In Mark 9:45 Jesus spoke of lost sinners being "cast into hell, into **the fire that never shall be quenched**." Paul articulated their fate as being "punished with **everlasting destruction** from the presence of the Lord, and from the glory of his power." (II Thessalonians 1:9). Finally, John "the Beloved" described the damned as being, "**tormented with fire and brimstone** in the presence of the holy angels, and in the presence of the Lamb: And the **smoke of their torment** ascendeth up for ever and ever: and they have no rest day nor night...." (Revelation 14:10-11)

According to a compilation of related Scriptures, other macabre characteristics of what unsaved men, women, boys, and girls will experience include: darkness; smoke; devils; worms; torture; isolation; despair; weeping; gnawing of tongues; gnashing of teeth; a perpetual falling sensation; permanent separation from God; and, strangely enough—as indicated by Abraham's words in Luke 16:25, "Son, **remember**...," —a *memory* that will haunt them throughout eternity, particularly by their recollections of how easily they *could* have been saved but foolishly rejected the Gospel. Thus, to the surprise of many, the lovely Lord Jesus Christ preached far more sermons about the pangs of Hell then He did about the glories of Heaven.

HELL WATERED DOWN BY MODERN RELIGION

Now the Bible specifically warns that in the "last days" (just before the end of the world as we know it, followed by the return of Christ) fewer and fewer people will be converted to Jesus (II Timothy 3:1-13). One of the main reasons why modern Americans are so flippant about eternity is that they rarely hear preaching on Hell anymore—the *ultimate incentive for* salvation (i.e., "Turn or burn!"). While twenty-first-century sinners may now find refuge in any number of Hell-denying "churches," such was not the case in our country's formative years.

Back in the day, when an unsaved person visited the local Baptist church, he was certain to hear, "If you don't git 'borned ag'in,' you'll split Hell *wide* open!" Petrified, he would run out of the building and flee into the First Presbyterian Church next door. Because this clerically adorned minister appeared more refined, the man was prone to lower his guard. However, this time the shocking message was, *"If you're not one of the elect,* you'll split Hell wide open, and—there's *nothing* you can do about it either!!"* Having staggered out the back door and across the street into the only other church in town, the poor wretch is last seen jumping out the window, followed by the Methodist parson screaming at the top of his lungs, "Even if you *are* saved, you can *still* lose it and split Hell wide open anyway!" Preaching like this kept a fledgling nation on the edge of the pew.

While the landmark English translation of the Holy Bible (i.e., the AV 1611, King James Version), specifically mentions Hell 53 times, a plethora of modern "Bibles" (inspired by Satan and profit-oriented publishers) have conveniently deleted 40 of these unsettling references. Accordingly, after John Lennon declared that the Beatles were more popular than Jesus Christ, he went on to desensitize his grateful fan base with the calming lyrics, "Imagine…no Hell below us…."

In 1979 Hank Williams, Jr., released his "iconic" number, "Whiskey Bent and Hell Bound." That same year (twelve months before Lennon's "imagination" morphed into reality "down below") the Australian rock band AC/DC unleashed their definitive hit, "Highway to Hell." The late serial killer Richard Ramirez (aka the "Night Stalker"), claimed "Highway to Hell" compelled him to murder his thirteen victims. When Mark Twain told about a dying man who couldn't decide as to which place to go, the iconic "humorist" remarked that both have their advantages, "Heaven for climate; Hell for company." Apparently, AC/DC agreed, as the first stanza of "Highway to Hell" concludes, "Goin' down; party time; *My friends are gonna be there, too, yeah.*"

For the record, the group's lead singer, Bon Scott, took his own exit ramp on February 19, 1980, having choked to death on his own vomit. Too bad ole Bon didn't heed the bumper sticker in front of him—

"THE PARTY IN HELL HAS BEEN CANCELLED DUE TO FIRE." No worries though, as a pint-sized, seven-year-old hombre named *Jesus* del Rio channeled his inner Bon Scott with a "crushing" rendition of "Highway to Hell" on a recent episode of the Spanish television show, *La Voz Kids* ("The Voice Kids"). Sadly, while the poor Hell-bound little rocker's braindead parents went apoplectic, the four judges rushed out of their chairs to mob their newest prodigy with hugs and kisses on stage.

Moving right along, Pete Rose (aka "Charlie Hustle"), legendary catcher for the Cincinnati Reds, ignorantly quipped, "I'd walk through Hell in a gasoline suit to play baseball." The Russian-born American writer and philosopher, Ayn Rand, flippantly stated, "When I die, I hope to go to Heaven, *whatever the Hell that is.*" Before taking her final breath, Academy Award-winner Joan Crawford reportedly snapped at the nurses praying at her bedside, "D—n it...Don't you *dare* ask God to help me!" Katharine Hepburn, who racked up a record four Oscars, boasted in a 1990 Associated Press interview, "I'm what is known as gradually disintegrating. I don't fear the next world, or anything. I don't fear Hell, and I don't look forward to Heaven." When Frank "I Did It My Way" Sinatra (aka "Ole Blue Eyes") kicked the bucket in 1998, he was buried with a bottle of Jack Daniels, a pack of Camels, a Zippo lighter, and a roll of dimes with which to "call his friends."

More recently, during the writing of this manuscript (2023), former California governor Arnold Schwarzenegger was asked about life after death in an interview with Danny DeVito for *Interview* magazine. The 75-year-old "Terminator" appropriately replied, "It reminds me of Howard Stern's question to me. 'Tell me, Governor, what happens to us when we die?' I said, 'Nothing. You're six feet under [i.e., *terminated*]. Anyone that tells you something else is a (blank)ing liar.'" (Included among these "liars" would be Arnie's creator, the Lord Jesus Christ.)

Of course, all these "fools" (as Psalm 14:1 labels them) gained their temporary inspiration from the Devil himself. In his seventeenth-century epic poem, "Paradise Lost," John Milton portrays Satan as saying, "Better to reign in Hell then serve in Heaven."

Nevertheless, no matter *how* macho sinners try to act, that "other place" is *always* in the back of their minds (Hebrews 2:15). The lyrics to the popular 1968 Blood, Sweat, and Tears song, "And When I Die," attest to this ubiquitous unnerving albatross: "I can swear there ain't no Heaven; *But I pray there ain't no Hell....*" (For the record, to make matters worse, the members of the iconic R&B band had nothing but scorn for the experience of God's Son in the Garden of Gethsemane, described in Luke 22:44 as, "...being in an **agony** he prayed more earnestly: and his **sweat** was as it were great drops of **blood** falling down to the ground.")

"THY SPEECH BEWRAYETH THEE"

When the Apostle Peter tried to deny his association with Jesus (following the Lord's arrest in the Garden), his detractors called him out due to his conspicuous Galilean brogue, "Surely thou also art one of them; for thy speech bewrayeth [archaic for betrays] thee." (Matthew 26:73) Similarly, while the possibility of anyone actually *going* to a literal Hell is never brought up in polite society, the subject remains imbedded in our national vocabulary. For instance, my late father grew up in "Hell's Kitchen," the tough Irish neighborhood on the West Side of Midtown Manhattan, New York. Butch Cassidy and the Sundance Kid roamed a particularly violent section of Fort Worth, Texas, called "Hell's Half Acre." In his epic poem, "The Charge of the Light Brigade," Alfred, Lord Tennyson wrote, "Into the mouth of Hell rode the six hundred." Audie Murphy's 1949 World War II memoir was entitled "To Hell and Back."

Harry S. Truman, America's no-nonsense thirty-third President, earned the moniker "Give 'em Hell Harry." The Protestant reformer Martin Luther once said, "I used to think that the Pope was the Vicar (representative) of Christ; now I think he's the Vicar of Hell." When the fire and brimstone Methodist evangelist Dr. Bob Jones, Sr., held a crusade in New York City, he shocked his audience by saying, "The only difference between New York and Hell is that New York is surrounded by water." When the sensational Prohibition-era evangelist Billy Sunday became irritated by the promiscuous way certain women were seated on the front row in one of his own meetings, he reportedly told them to "close the gates of Hell" (i.e., "keep your knees together"). More recently, the "Hells Angels" constitute the world's largest and most recognized "one percenter" outlaw motorcycle club, boasting a membership of over 6,000, with 467 chapters in 59 countries. In his 2016 presidential run, Donald Trump appealed to black voters by asking them, "What the Hell do you have to lose?"

Once again, while most people don't want to *hear* what the Bible says about Hell, they somehow manage to reference it on a daily basis! More than 100 well-known idioms about that infamous "Other Place" are all over the map. A short list of the most familiar colloquial expressions include: a cold day in Hell; when Hell freezes over; come Hell or high-water; the road to Hell is paved with good intentions; give someone holy Hell; scared the Hell out of someone; Hell hath no fury like a woman scorned; Hell on wheels; Hell-raiser; shot to Hell; Hell cat; Hell bent for leather; like a bat out of Hell; going to Hell in a handbasket; all Hell broke loose; a match made in Hell; what the Hell; for the Hell of it…ad nauseam.

HELL ON EARTH

Regarding another familiar idiom, "Hell on earth," believe it or not, such a place actually exists. Hell, Michigan, is an unincorporated township in Livingston County in the Great Lakes State. Established in 1838, roughly seventy people presently reside in Hell. (I once pastored a small church outside of Flint, Michigan, about sixty miles from Hell.) Locals still debate how it got such a devilish name. One theory posits that when the founder, George Reeves, was asked what the town should be called, he supposedly replied, "I don't care; you can call it 'Hell' for all I care." And so, they took him literally, the name becoming official on October 13, 1841.

To illustrate Paul's words in Romans 3:18, "There is no fear of God before their eyes," in 2019 the "Hell hole" of Hell, Michigan, was temporarily "purchased" by its pro-LGBT rights "mayor" (Elijah Daniel) and renamed "Gay Hell" (supposedly to protest President Trump's ban on American embassies flying pride flags). There is even a website (with a phone number) entitled, "SO, YOU WANT TO RULE HELL?" where aspiring candidates can pay a nominal fee to "become 'Mayor of Hell' for a day, or for an hour." On *Sunday*, April 24, 2022, an "historic" event took place in Hell; Jinx Sploinky Scoot—an infamous black cat, known for her bulging eyes and wobbly gait, not to mention sporting over 400,000 Instagram followers—was sworn in as mayor of Hell (even though she resides in California), holding the title until she was impeached that evening. (For what it's worth, the Blue State's current conservative minority would certainly make the connection between the "other place" and their own "hellcat" Democratic Governor, Gretchen Whitmer.)

Of course, Hell is *no* laughing matter, because once you arrive there, you *will* have "Hell to pay" in a "living Hell" and, like Rocky Valentine—you'll have a "snowball's chance in Hell" of ever escaping! Though Christmas Eve 2022 is officially known as "the day Hell froze over," with temperatures in the tiny Michigan town plunging to -25°C (-13°F), you won't find any popsicles in the *real* Hell! While the Northern general, William Tecumseh Sherman, famously said, "War is Hell," the Southern preacher, Bob Jones, Sr., stated more precisely, "War is God's judgment on the *living*, while Hell is God's judgment on the *dead*."

The most well-known secular piece of literature concerning Hell is the first part of the Italian writer Dante Alighieri's fourteenth-century epic poem, "Divine Comedy." However, of far greater significance, the most celebrated sermon in American history bore the politically incorrect title, "Sinners in the Hands of an Angry God." The quintessential revival known as the "Great Awakening" was ignited in Enfield, Connecticut, on July 8, 1741, when the Puritan theologian, Jonathan Edwards, unloaded his watershed message on his unsuspecting parishioners. Cultured New Englanders literally gripped the pews and cried out for mercy as the powerful preacher depicted their perilous predicament. "The God that holds you over the pit of Hell—much as one holds a spider or some loathsome insect over the fire—abhors you and is dreadfully provoked...You hang by a slender thread, with the flames of divine wrath flashing about it, and ready every moment to singe it and burn it asunder...."

THE "OTHER PLACE" IS THE "WRONG PLACE"

Evangelist D. L. Moody once made the astute observation, "This world is the closest thing to Hell that the *saved* will experience, and the closest thing to Heaven that the *lost* will ever experience." Perhaps the most arresting truth about the *real* "other place" is that it was never even created for man in the *first* place! In Matthew 25:41, Jesus tells the unsaved, "Depart from me, ye cursed, into everlasting fire, **prepared for the devil and his angels**."

God the Father did *everything* He possibly could to keep *you* from going there. *This included sacrificing His own Son on Calvary's Cross!* Thus, if you eventually land in Hell, you will have no one to blame but yourself. You see, having observed recalcitrant sinners reject Him at every turn in *this* life, God would *never* force them to spend eternity with Him in the *next* life. The only thing God is technically guilty of is honoring the free will of creatures that He made in His own image by permitting them to exercise their personal choice to deny Him.

One of the strangest verses in Scripture is Isaiah 5:14, "Therefore **hell hath enlarged herself**, and opened her mouth without measure...." As men and women continually reject the Gospel, God has to keep expanding that terrible place from its original, fixed size. Thus, to borrow another idiom—don't "*go* to Hell," for it's the "*wrong* place."

Finally, even "pure" Michiganders can distance themselves from the Lower Peninsula, by choosing to live in *Paradise,* an unincorporated community in Whitefish Township, some 342 miles due *north* of Hell—across the "Great Gulf" of the Mackinac Straits—in the Heavenly *Upper* Peninsula. And so, don't be like that foolish rich man in Luke 16 who will spend eternity muttering to himself, "The *Hell* if I know" (i.e., as to *why* he ever landed in a place that was never even intended for him). My friend, choose Jesus Christ so you won't ever have to hear those chilling last words: "Depart from me, ye cursed, into **everlasting fire**."

"Hell is truth seen too late."
(Thomas Hobbs)

7

What Must I Do To Be Saved?

WE HAVE NOW arrived at the pivotal seventh chapter of this book, containing the Bible answer to the eternal question, "What Must I Do to Be Saved?" Assuming that you are probably unfamiliar with the context of this divine encounter, a brief review is in order.

As previously noted on the "About the Cover" page, the Apostle Paul and his fellow laborer, Silas, were arrested in the Greek city of Philippi (their first missionary stop in Europe) for the "crime" of preaching the Gospel. After the magistrates had them severely beaten, they were remanded to the local jailer for safekeeping, "...who, having received such a charge, thrust them into the inner prison and made their feet fast in the stocks." (Acts 16:24)

However, as these men were not your average "cussing convicts," at midnight they began praying and singing praises to God (verse 25). Luke recorded what happened next: "And suddenly there was a great earthquake, so that the foundations of the prison were shaken: and immediately all the doors were opened, and everyone's bands were loosed" (verse 26). The startled jailer was jolted out of his sleep by the divine shockwave, then "...seeing the prison doors open, he drew out his sword, and would have killed himself, supposing that the prisoners had been fled" (verse 27). Many scholars believe this man was probably a retired veteran Roman soldier; therefore, suicide was instinctive, as a security breach on his watch was a capital offense for dereliction of duty.

But—*Hallelujah*—just in the nick of time, "...Paul cried with a loud voice, saying, Do thyself no harm: for we are all here" (verse 28). This turn of events sets the stage for the momentous question: "Then he called for a light, and sprang in, and came trembling, and fell down before Paul and Silas, And brought them out, and said, **Sirs, what must I do to be saved?**" (verses 29-30).

Friend, with absolutely *no* drama intended, *you* are now standing at the critical jumping off point of your own entire existence! *Where you will spend eternity is literally hanging in the balance.* Everything you have read in the previous six chapters was meant to prepare you to act upon Paul's answer in the next verse. (While the fact that you are *still* reading this book is phenomenal, coming close only counts in horseshoes and hand grenades.) Because you are just as important to God as that first-century jailer, the Apostle's message to him is equally applicable to you today! "And they said, **BELIEVE ON THE LORD JESUS CHRIST, and thou shalt be saved...**" (verse 31).

Thankfully, our story has a wonderful ending. The jailor is so blown away that he brings Paul and Silas into his own home; Luke continuing, "And they spake unto him the word of the Lord, and to all that were in his house" (verse 32). As the Bible teaches that the first step of obedience for any convert—*after they have been saved*—is to be immersed in water (Acts 2:41), the next verse shows that the unnamed corrections officer did indeed place his *faith* in Jesus Christ alone in order to be saved (followed by his entire family as well): "And he took them the same hour of the night, and washed their stripes; **and was baptized**, he and all his, straightway" (verse 33).

CONVICTION

Now, to make the all-important application to *your* situation, there are three interconnected scriptural elements to grasp. The first is known as "conviction." To illustrate, if you're driving over the speed limit and suddenly a police cruiser appears in your rearview mirror with lights flashing, you immediately come under "conviction;" i.e., you feel "convicted*"* that you are guilty (or, to revisit another one of those American idioms—guilty as "that *other* place").

Holy Ghost conviction is *the* necessary precursor to everyone's salvation experience. We see this by the jailor's reaction when he "...came **trembling**, and **fell down** before Paul and Silas." This inner "trembling" that wells up in a sinner's heart is something that God Himself causes when He knows that the individual is willing to be saved *if* he or she can only find the way. The key verse that describes this supernatural event is John 6:44 where Jesus says, "No man can come to me, except the Father which hath sent me **draw him…**" (i.e., like a fisherman draws a fish into his boat).

I once heard a seasoned evangelist say, "You can't get sinners *saved* until you first get them *lost!*" Another has said, "A swimmer won't call out for the lifeguard until a cramp convinces him or her that they are going under." Conviction is the Heaven-sent "cramp" that sets in simultaneously when sinners become convinced that they are in *big* trouble with God. For instance, by now you have read enough Bible in the prior chapters (along with my commentary) to realize that if you died today *you would split Hell wide open and fry like a Jimmy Dean sausage for eternity!* Assuming that you are a sincere person (and I certainly hope you are), that realization would be the equivalent of God lighting up *your* rearview mirror. Thus, as previously mentioned, that lesser-known second stanza in *Amazing Grace* says, "'Twas grace that taught my heart to *fear*; And grace my *fears* relieved…."

And so, as the Holy Spirit did with the Philippian jailer, He can employ any number of convicting factors to bring you to this critical hour of decision as well. For example, this man knew that Paul and Silas had something he did not possess, primarily when hearing them rejoicing after being severely beaten. He was also probably remorseful for the excessive manner in which he had obeyed his charge, having "**thrust** them into the inner prison…" (verse 24). Can you not think of the person who gave you this book and sense a similar longing to have the peace that they exhibit? How about any number of other men and women in your circle who have also testified to having gotten "saved" or "born-again," their transformed lives bearing witness to their words? When an atheist chided Reverend John Wesley, "Your followers are a bit too emotional," the eighteenth-century founder of the Methodist denomination replied, "You're probably right—but they die well!"

The jailer must also have recognized that something supernatural was occurring. Besides the midnight "Singspiration," there was the powerful earthquake, followed by those disconcerting words emanating from the darkness— "…for we are all here." Do you even realize how startling that statement must have been? The guard was about to kill himself because he was *convinced* that the prisoners had fled. Yet, to the contrary, while every inmate dreams of becoming an "outmate" at the first opportunity, after God blew their doors open, nobody (and I mean *nobody*) wanted to escape as bad as they thought they did! The silence was also deafening, for as anyone familiar with prison life knows, the greatest racket occurs in the night, with most inmates sleeping during the day. Here, however, they were *all* as quiet as church mice. (Psalm 91:5)

To apply this to your own situation, would you not agree (as mentioned in the "Introduction") that lately the Lord has been shaking up *your* world a bit more than usual? What size tremors has He been using to get *your* attention? (Surely, you don't want Him to send any additional aftershocks, do you?) Then, we have the beautiful providential connection. Amidst the holy terror of the moment, the jailer was undoubtedly captivated by the reality that these spiritual men had "somehow" wound up in *his* facility. Once again, the same goes for you: "Draw nigh to God, and **he will draw nigh to you**." (James 4:8) A popular hymn puts it this way:

> Once my soul was astray from the Heavenly way,
> I was wretched and as vile as could be;
> But my Savior in love gave me peace from above,
> **When he reached down his hand for me**.

All these factors taken together will produce a subconscious gratitude on your part. The jailer realized he *could* have taken his own life (not to mention he would have gone to Hell as well), *but* God intervened! How merciful has the Lord been to *you* in recent days? The key verse that will now transition us to our next point is Romans 2:4: "...not knowing that the **goodness of God** leadeth thee to **repentance**."

REPENTANCE

Whenever a lost sinner is under deep conviction, he or she is then ready to "repent." Most people conjure up the notion that "repentance" automatically has something to do with one "turning from their sins," etc. However, that *cannot* be the exclusive definition, any more than the so-called "Lord's prayer" *was* the "*Lord's* prayer," literally—for how could our sinless Saviour identify with His own petition in Luke 11:4, "And forgive us our **sins**...." Thus, we understand that Jesus was simply giving the Apostles an outline for *how* to pray.

In similar fashion, the King James Bible informs us that God Himself "repented" on several occasions (Genesis 6:6; I Chronicles 21:15; Jeremiah 26:13; Joel 2:13; Jonah 3:10). The explanation is simple. While under "normal" conditions, true repentance *will* generally result in some degree of turning *from* sin, the underlying Greek word for repentance (from which the English translation was made) is *metanoia,* which simply means "to change one's mind." Thus, if you check the aforementioned references, every instance of God "repenting" has to do with Him having changed *His* mind about something.

The rubber meets the road, however, when the Bible commands *humans* to "repent," specifically, unsaved men, women, boys, and girls. John the Baptist burst on the scene in the Judean wilderness, saying, "**Repent** ye: for the kingdom of heaven is at hand." (Matthew 3:2) Likewise, Jesus began His earthly mission by announcing, "I came not to call the righteous, but sinners to **repentance**." (Luke 5:32) In another sermon, Jesus told his listeners *twice,* "Except ye **repent**, ye shall all likewise perish." (Luke 13:3, 5) Later, in the Church Age, Paul testified that he preached to Jews and Gentiles alike "**repentance** toward God..." (Acts 20:21).

Although I Corinthians 2:14 says that an unsaved person is incapable of understanding the Bible in a general sense, God will make a slight exception when the subject matter involves one's personal salvation. For instance, near the end of John's gospel we read, "And many other signs truly did Jesus in the presence of his disciples, which are not written in this book: **But these are written, that you might believe that Jesus is the Christ, the Son of God; and that believing ye might have life through his name.**" (John 20:30-31) However, be that as it may, I wouldn't want to push the envelope by overloading my readers with too much theological material. (After all, this is the first book I have ever attempted to write for a target audience of God-fearing, though unsaved, folks.)

The role of Biblical repentance in your potential conversion is that you too must undergo a serious "change of mind." This bottom-line "change" involves your *attitude*—specifically, regarding the fact that your sin has alienated you from God! The prophet Isaiah thundered, "Behold, the LORD'S hand is not shortened, that it cannot save; neither his ear heavy, that it cannot hear: But your **iniquities** have **separated** between you and your God, and your **sins** have hid his face from you, that he will not hear:" (Isaiah 59:1-2)

Coming to this awareness—in concert with the price that God had to pay to cover your sin debt by punishing His own Son in your place—will normally trigger a complete metamorphosis of your *emotional* being. Jeremiah wrote "Mine eye affecteth mine heart...." (Lamentations 3:51) Thus, the first definition for "repentance" in the acclaimed *Webster's 1828 Dictionary* reads, "Sorrow for any thing done or said; the pain or grief which a person experiences in consequence of the injury or inconvenience produced by his own conduct." Notice how this matches Paul's inspired statement in II Corinthians 7:10, "For godly **sorrow** worketh **repentance** to salvation...."

Now when this proper attitude adjustment occurs, sinners will sense a natural change of mind about their individual sins. Before conviction, a lost person basically worships himself, as his or her own "god." (Thus, in II Thessalonians 2:4, Paul profiles the soon-coming "man of sin" as one, "Who opposeth and exalteth himself above all that is called God, or that is worshiped; so that he as God sitteth in the temple of God, showing himself that he is God.") While ministering in Lycaonia, Paul exhorted his listeners, saying, "Sirs, why do ye these things? We also are men of like passions with you, and preach unto you that ye should **turn** from these vanities unto the living God, which made heaven, and earth, and the sea, and all things that are therein." (Acts 14:15)

However, once they "see the light," a change of *action* will inevitably occur. Paul commended his converts for this very shift: "For they themselves shew of us what manner of entering in we had unto you, and how ye **turned to** God **from** idols to serve the living and true God...." (I Thessalonians 1:9) Anyone who says that repentance does *not* involve turning away from *some* sin has never read this passage, for how can one turn *to* God without turning *from* idolatry? And just for the record, regarding secular, material-minded Americans, Colossians 3:5 specifically defines "covetousness" as "idolatry."

The consummate evidence that a "convicted" sinner is finally ready to "repent" will be an unprecedented disposition to "do" *whatever* it takes to appease God's wrath (i.e., because of his or her sin). This great truth is expressed in the very question that the jailer asked— **"What must I do to be saved?"** The implication here is that he was absolutely willing to "do" *whatever* Paul told him. As a person's soul consists of a mind, emotion, and will, the process of repentance will involve all three components. Beginning with a change of *mind*, a change of *emotions* will follow, ending with the inevitable change of one's *will*. In the final analysis, repentance is reduced to nothing more than *a tired old sinner raising the white flag of surrender*—no longer wanting *his* or *her* will—but now desiring nothing but *God's* will!

The irony in the jailer's question, "What must I **do** to be saved?" is that there was absolutely *nothing* that he had to "do" (in a technical sense) but simply *believe* the Gospel. Paul described this surrender of the will as "the **obedience** of faith" (Romans 16:26) while conversely labeling the damned as those "that **obey not** the gospel of our Lord Jesus Christ" (II Thessalonians 1:8).

The greatest illustration I ever heard about repentance was the fictional antebellum story of a slave named Willy and his master, Mr. Jim. In the process of time, Willy got born-again and exhibited a radical transformation in his life (II Corinthians 5:17). After observing Willy for some time, Mr. Jim decided to look into this phenomenon, as he was burdened down with many private heartaches at the time. Consequently, he went to the shanty slave quarters and knocked on Willy's door. When the master asked his chattel how he could have the same joy and peace that he possessed, Willy simply smiled and said, "Follow me, Boss."

Willy then led the enquiring sinner over to the nearby hog pen and gave him the following bizarre instructions. "Well, Mr. Jim, if'n you really wants to get saved, den you gots to put on dat fancy white suit dat you loves so much, along with yo' white shirt, white tie, white socks, white shoes, and white hat—dat one with da white feather—den, you gots to climb up on da top of dis here fence and dive *plum* into dat dere slop!" Predictably, the dignified plantation owner recoiled in shock at such a preposterous proposal and promptly returned to his mansion, uttering several expletives along the way.

However, the more he tried to repress Willy's hog pen from his mind, the more agitated ("convicted") he grew in his despair. The fact that a smiling Willy kept reminding him that he was praying for his soul every time they would meet didn't help matters, either. And so, late one night Willy was again awakened by a knock on his door. When he opened it, there stood his proud master—all decked out in his white suit, white shirt, white tie, white socks, white shoes, and white hat (the one with the white feather).

The two men immediately proceeded to the smelly pigsty, whereupon Mr. Jim gingerly mounted the wobbly fence. He then assumed the position that a swimmer does when he is about to dive into the pool. Finally, at the very last moment, with perspiration pouring off his face, he sheepishly asked, "Willy, are you *sure* I have to do this in order to get saved?" With his master's ridiculous profile testifying to his having raised the white flag of surrender, Willy smiled and said, "Naw sir, Mr. Jim; you don't gots to dive into dat slop—you just gots to be *willin'*!"

BELIEF

The essence of Paul's answer to the jailer's question was based on the sacred text in John 3:16: "For God so loved the world, that he gave his only begotten Son, that whosoever **believeth in him** shall not perish, but have everlasting life." Yet, note how the Apostle summarized his public ministry by linking repentance *to* faith, "And how I kept back nothing that was profitable unto you, but have shewed you, and have taught you publicly, and from house to house, Testifying both to the Jews, and also to the Greeks, **repentance** toward God, **and faith** toward our Lord Jesus Christ." (Acts 20:20-21) Thus, we see that "repentance *and* faith" represent two sides of the same coin.

When a sinner raises that white flag of surrender, he or she is essentially coming clean with theirself—acknowledging that they no longer want to do *their* thing, but rather *God's* thing. In the well-known parable about the "Prodigal Son," Jesus described the moment of truth for the repentant profligate accordingly: "And when he **came to himself**, he said, How many hired servants of my father's have bread enough and to spare, and I perish with hunger! **I will arise and go to my father**...." (Luke 15:17-18)

At that point, the Holy Spirit takes over and informs the person that the *first* thing He wants is for them to get saved by placing their faith in "the Gospel" (defined in I Corinthians 15:3-4 as the death, burial, and resurrection of Jesus Christ). Consequently, the trembling jailer was instructed, **"Believe** on the Lord Jesus Christ and thou shalt be saved...." However, notice that I said, "the *first* thing God wants." While there is only *one* thing, and *one* thing alone, that a person must "do" to be saved, which is *believe* on Jesus Christ, there *are* many additional things that God wants a person to do *after* he or she gets saved to live a consecrated Christian life for Him. Thus, Paul told his listeners that they "should **repent** and turn to God, and do **works** meet [suitable or right] for **repentance**." (Acts 26:20)

The best proof that that a person was sincere when they initially trusted Christ, would be their subsequent efforts to please the Lord. II Corinthians 5:17 states, "Therefore if any man be in Christ, he is a **new creature**: old things are passed away; behold, all things are become new. **And all things are of God**, who hath reconciled us to himself by Jesus Christ, and hath given to us the ministry of reconciliation;" The main difference between a true "possessor" and a mere "professor" is that the former will display his (or her) gratitude by desiring to live for God after salvation! Thus, a common Bible Belt expression says, "Watch out for those 'converts' who ask Jesus to save them on *Saturday* and the FBI can't find them on *Monday*." The New Testament pattern is found in Acts 2:41-42, "Then they that gladly received his word were baptized... And they **continued** steadfastly in the apostles' doctrine and fellowship, and in breaking of bread, and in prayers."

GOOD NEWS AND BAD NEWS

The saying goes, "I've got some *good* news and some *bad* news." As noted earlier in this chapter, the good news is that you are *still* reading this book! In case you would like to know why—it's because a literal miracle is taking place!! Because God knows that you are searching for the truth, He is literally helping you to find it. Like He states in Jeremiah 29:13, "And ye shall seek me, and find me, **when ye shall search for me with all your heart**."

According to the book of Acts, the first Gentile in Europe to become a Christian was a religious business woman. Notice what God did for *her*, because Acts 16:13 reveals she was participating in a prayer meeting when Paul and his team came upon her: "And a certain woman named Lydia, a seller of purple, of the city of Thyatira, which worshiped God, heard us: **whose heart the Lord opened, that she attended unto the things which were spoken of Paul**." (Acts 16:14) This divine intervention illustrates the precise meaning of John 1:12— "But as many as received him, to them gave he **power** to become the sons of God, even to them that believe on his name...."

She then went on to manifest the evidence of her sincerity by opening her home to serve as the first New Testament church on the Continent: "And when she was baptized, and her household, she besought us, saying, **If ye have judged me to be faithful to the Lord**, come into my house, and abide there. And she constrained us." (Acts 16:15)

You say, "Preacher, well, what's the *bad* news?" The answer is twofold; not only will you *still* go straight to a Devil's Hell if you don't *act* on your newly found knowledge (i.e., about how to be saved), but your eternal punishment will now be *hotter* than it would have been if you hadn't learned anything. This is because God holds men accountable for the light that He gives them. Jesus said in Luke 12:28, "For unto whomsoever much is given, of him shall be much required...." Thus, back in the day, the old-time preachers would say, "Light rejected becomes *lightning!*"

SO—WHAT WILL *YOU* DO THEN WITH JESUS?

When Jesus appeared before Pilate's judgment seat, the Roman governor asked the bloodthirsty mob, **"What shall I do then with Jesus which is called Christ?"** (Matthew 27:22) This is the same question that the Holy Spirit is asking *you* this very moment. You only have two possible answers. After Paul concluded his Gospel presentation to the Jews in Rome, Luke relates, "And **some believed** the things which were spoken, and **some believed not**." (Acts 28:24)

To conclude this watershed seventh chapter, if *you* want to "get saved" *God's* way, you will have to "do" exactly what the Philippian jailer did— **"believe** on the Lord Jesus Christ," *period*. This simply means that you make a conscious, heartfelt decision to take God at His word. For as we have previously seen, Jesus has already paid your sin debt at Calvary, perfectly *propitiating* ("appeasing") His Father's wrath (Romans 3:25; I John 2:2). As Ephesians 1:7 attests, this appeasement was perfected by the shed blood of Christ: "In whom we have **redemption through his blood**, the forgiveness of sins, according to the riches of his grace...."

The decisiveness of this vicarious atonement was immortalized by those three succinct words our Saviour uttered from the Cross: "It is **finished**." (John 19:30) Therefore, you don't have to pay for your own sins (by burning in Hell forever). All you have to "do" is accept the divine *gift* that's been freely offered to you. "For the wages of sin is death; but the **gift of God** is eternal life through Jesus Christ our Lord." (Romans 6:23)

On a technical note, this holy transaction is consummated by simple *faith*. Thus, Ephesians 2:8 states, "For by grace are ye saved through **faith**...." However, many Christians (myself included) will testify that they were born-again by personally *asking* Jesus to save them via the so-called "sinner's prayer." While they couldn't possibly have discerned such spiritual nuances at the time (as you probably cannot either), they simply attached an *outward* "audible petition" to their *inward* "silent decision" (i.e., to believe).

The best-known Scripture for this correlation is Romans 10:13, "For whosoever shall **call** upon the name of the Lord shall be saved." The preceding verses in Romans 10:9-10 set the context: "That if thou shalt **confess with thy mouth** the Lord Jesus, **and shalt believe in thine heart** that God hath raised him from the dead, **thou shalt be saved**. For with the **heart** man **believeth** unto righteousness; and with the **mouth confession** is made unto salvation."

And so, seeing that you'll be talking to Jesus for the rest of your Christian life, I'm *sure* that the One who said in John 6:37, "...him that **cometh to me** I will in **no** wise cast out," wouldn't mind your *initiating* things by "coming to Him" via a simple prayer (i.e., to acknowledge that you want to accept His offer by faith). At least, this is the way Jesus described how things went down with that "IRS agent" in Luke 18:13, "And the publican [tax collector], standing afar off, would not lift up so much as his eyes unto heaven, but smote upon his breast, **saying**, God be merciful to me a sinner." Another classic illustration is the dying thief, who cried unto Jesus, "Lord, **remember me** when thou comest into thy kingdom." (Luke 23:42) The truth is, your "prayer" is the initial evidence that you truly got saved in the first place—that you *have* believed the Gospel: "For whosoever shall call upon the name of the Lord shall be saved. **How then shall they call on him in whom they have not believed?**" (Romans 10:13,14) This was the very proof the Lord offered to Ananias that the frightening Saul of Tarsus (soon to become the Apostle Paul) had been genuinely converted, "...for, behold, he prayeth...." (Acts 9:11)

Regarding my earlier illustration of a drowning swimmer calling out to the lifeguard, my closing appeal would be for you to review the account of Peter having his own water emergency while stutter-stepping on the Sea of Galilee. According to Matthew 14:30-31, "But when he saw the wind boisterous, he was **afraid**; and **beginning to sink**, he **cried**, saying, **Lord, save me**. And **immediately** Jesus stretched forth his hand, and **caught him…**" The spiritual application is clear; if you will *call* on Him, He will save *you* immediately too!!

To reiterate for emphasis, *the* single thing that will save you from Hell is a conscious, *heartfelt* decision to trust Christ as your personal Saviour. While communicating this desire to the Lord by a simple prayer is not wrong, it is the *faith* behind the prayer that cements the conversion. As Jesus warned in Matthew 7:21-23, there will be plenty of religious people in Hell who had prayed some mechanical prayer—but *without* possessing sincere faith. "**Not every one that saith unto me, Lord, Lord, shall enter into the kingdom of heaven…**Many will say to me in that day, Lord, Lord, have we not prophesied in thy name? and in thy name have cast out devils? and in thy name done many wonderful works? And then will I profess unto them, **I never knew you**: depart from me, ye that work iniquity."

In closing, as previously mentioned, when the disciples asked Jesus, "Lord, teach us to pray…," He graciously gave them a sample prayer to follow (Luke 11:1). On August 25, 1974, at the conclusion of the Sunday morning service at the Marcus Hook Baptist Church in Lynwood, Pennsylvania, I left my pew and went forward to tell the pastor that I wanted to be saved, whereupon a deacon took me into a side room and showed me the same Scriptures that I've shared with you. I then exercised *my* desire to trust Christ by uttering a simple "sinner's prayer," like the sample one below. And so, my dear friend—if *you* want to receive Jesus as *your* personal Lord and Saviour—*won't you do so this very moment by uttering a similar heartfelt petition like this?*

"Dear Lord, I know that I am a sinner, and if I died right now, I would go straight to Hell. But I believe that you died for me and that you were buried and rose again from the grave. Right now, as best as I know how, I want you to become my personal Saviour and take me to Heaven when I die. Amen."

> "**Come unto me**, all ye that labour and are heavy laden,
> and I will give you rest….and him that **cometh**
> **to me** I will in **no** wise cast out."
> (Matthew 11:28; John 6:37)

8

Eternal Security

ASSUMING THAT YOU placed your trust in Jesus Christ by the end of chapter seven, you are now what the Bible calls a "born-again" Christian (John 3:3-5). This means that you will be reading *this* chapter through a set of transformed eyes (Ephesians 1:18). John told the apostate Laodiceans in Revelation 3:18 to "anoint thine eyes with eyesalve, that thou mayest see." (As a timely "coincidence," in Bible numerology, *seven* represents God's perfect number, while *eight* represents new beginnings.) Thus, Paul wrote in II Corinthians 5:17-18, "**Therefore if any man be in Christ, he is a new creature**: old things are passed away; **behold, all things are become new**. And all things are of God, who hath reconciled us to himself by Jesus Christ, and hath given to us the ministry of reconciliation."

Many other Scriptures attest to your new-found spiritual status *in* Christ. For instance, John 5:24 describes you and me as having "passed **from** death **unto** life." According to Colossians 1:13, God the Father "...hath delivered us **from** the power of darkness, and hath translated us **into** the kingdom of his dear Son." Romans 8:1 says, "There is therefore now no condemnation to them which are **in** Christ Jesus, who walk not after the flesh, but after the Spirit."

Though the religious world remains clueless, the Bible affirms that any man, woman, boy, or girl who accepts Jesus Christ as their personal Lord and Saviour receives "eternal life" *that very moment* (i.e., this marvelous gift becomes your *immediate* possession by the good grace of God). Thus, John 3:18 says, "He that **believeth** on him **is not condemned**," while verse 36 adds, "He that **believeth** on the Son **hath** everlasting life...." I John 5:12 says the same: "He that **hath** the Son

hath life; and he that **hath not** the Son of God **hath not** life." (Notice how all these verbs appear in the *present* tense.)

The most important facet of this supernatural transition is that the very nature of *"eternal* life" means you can *never* lose it. Theologically speaking, this is known as the doctrine of "Eternal Security" (or as Satan's crowd derisively labels it, "Once saved, always saved"). Consider the words of Jesus, "My sheep hear my voice, and I know them, and they follow me: **and I give unto them eternal life; and they shall never perish**, neither shall any man pluck them out of my hand. My Father, which gave them me, is greater than all; **and no man is able to pluck them out of my Father's hand.** I and my Father are one." (John 10:27-30) Like the black preacher put it— "His grip don't slip!"

The greatest proof text on eternal security is I John 5:13, "These things have I written unto you that believe on the name of the Son of God; **that ye may know that ye have eternal life**, and that ye may believe on the name of the Son of God."

As an evangelist, I travel and preach all over the country. Whenever I arrive at my appointed destination, I simply walk into the motel lobby and the desk clerk hands me my room key. Not only was the reservation made ahead of time, but the bill has been paid in full by the host pastor. The same applies to our future home in Heaven. Jesus told His followers: "Let not your heart be troubled: ye believe in God, believe also in me. In my Father's house are many mansions: if it were not so, I would have told you. **I go to prepare a place for you.**" (John 14:1-2) Thus, Paul could testify, "We are confident, I say, and willing rather to be absent from the body, and to be present with the Lord. (II Corinthians 5:8)

The main reason that sinners are truly "saved" by simply believing the Gospel is because the third member of the Trinity literally enters their bodies at conversion! Paul wrote in I Corinthians 3:16, "Know ye not that ye are the temple of God, **and that the Spirit of God dwelleth in you?**" In a more extended passage, the Apostle delineates the very sequence of our salvation experience, likening the indwelling of the Holy Ghost to earnest money used to secure a real estate transaction: "That we should be to the praise of his glory, **who first trusted in Christ.** In whom ye also trusted, **after that ye heard the word of truth,** the gospel of your salvation: in whom also **after that ye believed, ye were sealed with that holy Spirit of promise,** which is the **earnest of our**

inheritance until the redemption of the purchased possession, unto the praise of his glory." (Ephesians 1:12-14)

The sudden realization that you can *never* go to "The Other Place" constitutes the main source of the believer's joy. Thus, Romans 5:1 states, "Therefore being justified by faith, **we have peace with God** through our Lord Jesus Christ." Notice how Luke describes the Philippian jailer similarly, "And when he had brought them into his house, he set meat before them, and **rejoiced**, believing in God with all his house." (Acts 16:34) This perfectly reflects our Lord's twofold mission statement: "I am come that they might have **life, and** that they might have **it** more **abundantly**." (John 10:10) Not only does Jesus provide saved sinners with *eternal* life (i.e., in the "sweet by and by"), but also with *abundant* life (in the "nasty now and now").

Because of this, you must always remember that the Devil will hound you till the day you die. (Why do you think Paul and Silas *wound* up *locked* up in the first place?) Satan's "Plan A" was to keep you from *getting* saved. However, now that you've wrecked *that* goal (i.e., by trusting Christ), "Plan B" is to keep you from *growing* in your new faith. The main way "Ole Smutty Face" will try to rob you of your joy is to make you think you can become lost again (i.e., whenever you sin after your conversion). On the contrary, Scripture teaches that all born-again Christians sin after their salvation (Romans 7:15; I John 1:8,10).

But the reason we don't **lose** our salvation is because we **didn't do** anything to **earn** it in the first place (Galatians 3:1-3). Thus, not only does Jesus do the initial saving, but He *keeps* us saved as well. Paul wrote in II Timothy 1:12, "...for I know whom I have believed, and am persuaded that **he is able to keep** that which I have committed unto him against that day." Satan will always try to get *saved* people to think they're *lost* (I Corinthians 12:3) while trying to get *lost* people to think they're *saved* (Matthew 7:21-23).

What we *are* told to do is to confess any act of disobedience in order to maintain our *fellowship* with God, not our *relationship* with Him. The key cross-reference for this truth is I John 1:9, "**If we confess our sins,** he is faithful and just to forgive us our sins, and to cleanse us from all unrighteousness." Should we refuse to "get right," our Heavenly Father will spank us accordingly: "For whom the Lord loveth he chasteneth, and scourgeth every son whom he receiveth." (Hebrews 12:6) Notice how the writer goes on in verse nine to compare our new spiritual rapport with

God to the actions of any responsible human disciplinarian. "Furthermore we have had fathers of our flesh which corrected us, and we gave them reverence: shall we not much rather be in subjection unto the Father of spirits, and live?"

And so, now that you have a handle on the *fact* that you *can* be 100% sure of going straight to *Heaven* when you die—because you are "sealed" more securely than your granny's jars of green beans—the following chapter will tell you what you have to do in order to secure that "*abundant* life" while you're living down here on *Earth*!

"For I am persuaded, that neither death, nor life, nor angels,
nor principalities, nor powers, nor things present, nor things to
come, Nor height, nor depth, nor any other creature,
shall be able to separate us from the love of God,
which is in Christ Jesus our Lord."
(Romans 8:38-39)

9

What To Do After You Get Saved

WHEN JESUS WAS headed to the Garden of Gethsemane, He told His disciples, "I am the vine, ye are the branches: He that abideth in me, and I in him, the same bringeth forth much **fruit**: for without me ye can do nothing." (John 15:5) To revisit our study on Bible numerics, the number "nine" represents *fruit bearing* (i.e., Abraham was *ninety-nine* years old when Isaac was born; Sarah was *ninety*; a mother's gestation period lasts *nine* months...*nine* letters in Holy Bible; Scripture; Word of God; King James; 1611, 1+6+1+1=9; etc.) Thus, Galatians 5, verses 22-23 (2+2+2+3=9) lists the *nine* "**fruit of the Spirit**" as *nine* spiritual traits: "love, joy, peace, longsuffering, gentleness, goodness, faith, meekness, temperance." Therefore, our *ninth* chapter will review what the Bible says you must do if you want to become a *fruitful* Christian, for as Jesus told His own, "Herein is my Father glorified, that ye bear much fruit...." (John 15:8)

In chapter seven we established that Bible repentance (for humans) constitutes a "change of mind" that results in a concurrent, heartfelt surrender of *our* will to *God's* will (I Thessalonians 1:9-10). The key proof text is Acts 20:21 where Paul summarized his public ministry as proclaiming "**repentance** toward God, and **faith** toward our Lord Jesus Christ." As we also noted, the quintessential illustration for this soul-saving moment constitutes the metaphorical raising of a white flag, exhibited by the jailer's question in Acts 16:30, "**What** must I **do** to be saved?" (Like ole Willy said— "You just gots to be *willin'*.")

The bottom line in all of this reverts back to something else we said. When a convicted sinner has truly repented (by raising that white flag) and subsequently desires *God's* will for his life, the Lord's expanded answer—in order—is that, first of all, He wants that person to get saved (i.e., by trusting His Son as Saviour). Then, after that, there are several *more* things that He wants as well, all of which are necessary for the new believer to grow in his or her spiritual life. Consequently, the best evidence that you have been gloriously saved is your immediate desire to take these additional steps (Acts 2:41-42; I Corinthians 12:3).

WATER BAPTISM

Your first priority upon trusting Jesus Christ as Saviour is to bear an *outward* witness to that *inner* decision. Acts 2:41 states, "Then they that gladly received his word were **baptized**." Immediately after Lydia's conversion, Luke records that **"...she was baptized...."** (Acts 16:15) As we have previously noted, when the Philippian jailer brought Paul and Silas into his home, **"...the same hour of the night** [he] washed their stripes **and was baptized**, he and all his, straightway." (Acts 16:33)

While different religions employ a variety of modes (i.e., affusion; aspersion; partial immersion; as well as pedobaptism, the sprinkling of infants, also known as christening), suffice it to say that the only proper manner given in Scripture is total immersion in deep water by a candidate who is old enough to have made a conscious decision to trust Christ (Acts 8:39). Furthermore, this can only be authoritatively administered under the auspices of a local New Testament Church (I Corinthians 11:2). This means that your "well-intentioned" Mormon truck-driver uncle cannot dunk you in his bathtub, etc.

Bible baptism pictures two great truths: one you can understand now, and one you will have to wait awhile to comprehend. The three-fold position of you standing *upright* in the water, then being lowered *under* the water, and then raised up *from* the water symbolizes to all who are witnessing the ordinance that you have trusted the *death, burial*, and *resurrection* of Jesus Christ. I have often used a wedding band to illustrate baptism. While you do not have to wear one to *be* married, you must do so if you want people to *know* that you are married. (I have the precious memory of being baptized on Christmas Eve in 1974.) However, the deeper truth is that your *visible* immersion *after* your conversion pictures the *invisible* reality that you were baptized *into* Jesus Christ *at* your conversion: "For by one Spirit are we all **baptized** into one body...." (I Corinthians 12:13)

CHURCH MEMBERSHIP

As you start your new life in Jesus, you need to realize that you are extremely vulnerable as a baby Christian. Because Satan will try to discourage, confuse, and abuse you from the outset, it is imperative that you flee to the one main refuge God has prepared to sustain you—the local New Testament Church. While there are many so-called "churches" to choose from, *the* one you want to find is a Bible-believing, "King James Only," Independent Baptist Church, one that "rightly divides" the Scripture. Now, obviously, you cannot possibly grasp the meaning of all these terms at this point; that is why I've given you these guidelines to follow by faith, *until* you *can* grasp their significance.

There are many spiritual benefits to being in a good local assembly; first and foremost would be having a loving shepherd to help you grow in your faith. In Jeremiah 3:15, the Lord said, "And I will give you pastors according to mine heart, which shall feed you with knowledge and understanding." Paul told the Ephesian believers that pastors (and evangelists) were God's special gift to the churches (Ephesians 4:11-13). The "sheep" are therefore exhorted: "Obey them that have the rule over you, and submit yourselves: for they watch for your souls, as they that must give account...." (Hebrews 13:17)

Another important benefit of faithfully attending the right kind of church is to have fellowship with likeminded believers. Hebrews 10:25 enjoins, "Not forsaking the assembling of ourselves together, as the manner of some is; but **exhorting one another**: and so much the more, as ye see the day approaching." Whenever a single piece of coal is removed from a grill, it inevitably goes out. The same is true for the Christian, for they too will languish without the support group of other "briquettes." And with the world about to implode, this need for spiritual camaraderie is stronger than ever. (As a practical suggestion, to help find the right church, you might consider asking the person who gave you this book.)

KING JAMES BIBLE

You say, "Dr. Grady, but what in the world does that earlier statement of yours mean about 'being baptized into one spirit?'" Well, as I already mentioned, that second, deeper picture of baptism is something that you will have to learn about later (i.e., after you have become grounded on the basics). Which brings up the critical necessity of your acquiring, reading, studying, and meditating upon the Holy Bible. As Jesus likened our conversion to a "second birth" (John 3:3-5), notice how Peter continues the metaphor by comparing an infant's instinctive craving for his mother's milk to a "baby" Christian's need for the "milk" of Scripture: "As newborn babes, desire the **sincere milk of the word**, that ye may grow thereby." (I Peter 2:2)

While one of the main functions of a pastor is to help you learn *how* to study your Bible (along with "feeding" you through his weekly sermons), the greater responsibility will be for *you* to develop your own life-long relationship with "*the* Book" that God used to birth you into your new life in Christ. And *the* single most important factor here is to acquire the correct English translation—the King James Bible (also known as the 1611 Authorized Version). The particular reasons why this is the *only* Bible you should ever read is another one of those heavier subjects that you will learn in time. (And don't get tricked into buying a *New King James Version;* make sure it's the original King James Version.)

PRAYER

Someone has said that when we *read* the Bible, God talks to us; when we *pray*, we talk to God. Another has said that Jeremiah 33:3 is the Lord's telephone number: "Call unto me, and I will answer thee, and show thee great and mighty things, which thou knowest not." Paul wrote, "Be careful for nothing; but in every thing by prayer and supplication with thanksgiving let your requests be made known unto God. And the peace of God, which passeth all understanding, shall keep your hearts and minds through Christ Jesus." (Philippians 4:6-7)

While the very concept of the created being communicating with his or her Creator may seem disconcerting at first, the Apostle John assures us, "And this is the **confidence** that we have in him, that, if we ask any thing according to his will, **he heareth us**." (I John 5:14) Thus, Hebrews 4:16 says, "Let us therefore come boldly unto the throne of grace, that we may obtain mercy, and find grace to help in time of need." And remember, always pray in Jesus's name. "And whatsoever you shall ask **in my name**, that will I do, that the Father may be glorified in the Son." (John 14:13) We have no merit of our own; we can only approach God in prayer through Jesus Christ.

There are many other important priorities that you will need to learn as well. A shortlist would include: witnessing to others about Jesus (Acts 1:8); taking the Lord's Supper (I Corinthians 11:26); striving to live a holy life (II Corinthians 6:14-17); fasting (Matthew 6:16-18); supporting your local church financially (Malachi 3:10); et al. However, this introduction will get you started until you can catch up with the other areas after you get grounded in a good local assembly with a devoted shepherd.

10

A Final Caution

HOPEFULLY, BY NOW you have trusted Jesus Christ as your personal Lord and Saviour, for the Bible explicitly warns sinners not to procrastinate regarding such a critical decision. In I Corinthians 6:2, Paul enjoined his readers, "...behold, **now** is the accepted time; behold, **now** is the day of salvation." Hebrews 3:7 similarly states, "...To day if ye will hear his voice, Harden not your hearts...."

The obvious reason why people should get saved at their earliest opportunity is because none of us know when death may call. David said in I Samuel 20:3, "...there is but a step between me and death." While Proverbs 27:1 says, "Boast not thyself of to morrow; for thou knowest not what a day may bring forth," James 4:14 adds, "Whereas ye know not what shall be on the morrow. For what is your life? It is even a vapour, that appeareth for a little time, and then vanisheth away."

On the other hand, if you have *not* accepted Christ thus far, any number of reasons would account for this extremely dangerous situation. One of the primary causes for delay often involves the unpleasant scenario where the prospect's loved one has passed away—*without* being born-again. (The Devil *loves* to play mind games with this one.) Thus, to accept the Gospel, he or she must also be willing to accept the reality that their relative is burning in Hell.

To illustrate, while pastoring in Michigan, I witnessed to a building contractor who subsequently made a "profession" of faith. However, though he briefly attended my Sunday morning services (sleeping through most of the sermon), he never would get baptized—a pretty good scriptural indicator (based on Acts 2:41) that he didn't get saved in the first place. I quickly surmised that the stumbling block was that his son, a proselyte of the Church of Jesus Christ of Latter-day Saints (Mormons), had recently committed suicide. On a personal note, when I was eleven years old, my Lutheran mother took her life as well. Sadly, I have no recollection of her ever saying she had been saved.

PRAYER IN HELL

This Satanic stratagem is why older Roman Catholics are so difficult to win, especially among the staunchest ethnic groups (Italians, Poles, Latinos, et al.). To bump Jesus and His Cross ahead of Mary and her rosary beads is to consign one's mama (and grandmother) to the Lake of Fire. (Jews are even *harder* to reach.)

However, while definitely a bitter pill to swallow, there *is* a scriptural answer to this conundrum in Luke 16:24-31. As we have previously observed, when the rich man wound up in Hell, his first petition was for Abraham to "...send Lazarus, that he may dip the tip of his finger in water, and cool my tongue; for I am tormented in this flame." Sadly, as we also learned, Abraham informed him that any respite was now out of the question.

At this point, notice what the rich man requests next: "**Then** he said, I **pray** thee therefore, father, that thou wouldest **send him to my father's house**: For I have five brethren; **that he may testify unto them**, lest they also come into this place of torment." (As an insightful aside, although the rich man was too busy for prayer while on earth, down below he has *plenty* of time to pray.) Yet, once again, Abraham declines, stating that as these lost siblings already have "Moses and the prophets" (i.e., the Old Testament), "...let them hear them."

The rich man's inane reply constitutes one of the strangest statements in all of Scripture: "**Nay**, father Abraham: but if one went unto them from the dead, they will **repent**." While this wealthy, self-willed Jew went to Hell for his stiff-necked resistance to God's word, notice how he *still* believes he knows more than Father Abraham! By the way, it is also worth noting that while some Christians downplay the doctrine of *repentance*, the doomed in the abyss are more than acquainted with its relevance.

The obvious takeaway in all of this—should Satan try to lay a similar eleventh-hour guilt trip on you—is that *your* tormented loved ones would *also* want you to get saved exactly like the rich man wanted *his* five brethren to do what *he* never did!! One day we we'll discover where those five men went when they died. But in the meantime— make sure that *you* wind up where Lazarus is this very moment.

"We are confident, I say, and willing rather to be
absent from the body, and to be present with the Lord."
(II Corinthians 5:8)

God bless you my dear friend...
And be *sure* to e-mail me about your decision to trust Christ!

"The entrance of thy words giveth light;
it giveth understanding unto the simple."

(Psalm 119:130)

THE GOSPEL ACCORDING TO
ST. JOHN

IN the beginning was the Word, and the Word was with God, and the Word was God.

2 The same was in the beginning with God.

3 All things were made by him; and without him was not any thing made that was made.

4 In him was life; and the life was the light of men.

5 And the light shineth in darkness; and the darkness comprehended it not.

6 ¶ There was a man sent from God, whose name *was* John.

7 The same came for a witness, to bear witness of the Light, that all *men* through him might believe.

8 He was not that Light, but *was sent* to bear witness of that Light.

9 *That* was the true Light, which lighteth every man that cometh into the world.

10 He was in the world, and the world was made by him, and the world knew him not.

11 He came unto his own, and his own received him not.

12 But as many as received him, to them gave he power to become the sons of God, *even* to them that believe on his name:

13 Which were born, not of blood, nor of the will of the flesh, nor of the will of man, but of God.

14 And the Word was made flesh, and dwelt among us, (and we beheld his glory, the glory as of the only begotten of the Father,) full of grace and truth.

15 ¶ John bare witness of him, and cried, saying, This was he of whom I spake, He that cometh after me is preferred before me: for he was before me.

16 And of his fulness have all we received, and grace for grace.

17 For the law was given by Moses, *but* grace and truth came by Jesus Christ.

18 No man hath seen God at any time; the only begotten Son, which is in the bosom of the Father, he hath declared *him*.

19 ¶ And this is the record of John, when the Jews sent priests and Levites from Jerusalem to ask him, Who art thou?

20 And he confessed, and denied not; but confessed, I am not the Christ.

21 And they asked him, What then? Art thou Elias? And he saith, I am not. Art thou that prophet? And he answered, No.

22 Then said they unto him, Who art thou? that we may give an answer to them that sent us. What sayest thou of thyself?

23 He said, I *am* the voice of one crying in the wilderness, Make straight the way of the Lord, as said the prophet Esaias.

24 And they which were sent were of the Pharisees.

25 And they asked him, and said unto him, Why baptizest thou then, if thou be not that Christ, nor Elias, neither that prophet?

26 John answered them, saying,

I baptize with water: but there standeth one among you, whom ye know not;

27 He it is, who coming after me is preferred before me, whose shoe's latchet I am not worthy to unloose.

28 These things were done in Bethabara beyond Jordan, where John was baptizing.

29 ¶ The next day John seeth Jesus coming unto him, and saith, Behold the Lamb of God, which taketh away the sin of the world.

30 This is he of whom I said, After me cometh a man which is preferred before me: for he was before me.

31 And I knew him not: but that he should be made manifest to Israel, therefore am I come baptizing with water.

32 And John bare record, saying, I saw the Spirit descending from heaven like a dove, and it abode upon him.

33 And I knew him not: but he that sent me to baptize with water, the same said unto me, Upon whom thou shalt see the Spirit descending, and remaining on him, the same is he which baptizeth with the Holy Ghost.

34 And I saw, and bare record that this is the Son of God.

35 ¶ Again the next day after John stood, and two of his disciples;

36 And looking upon Jesus as he walked, he saith, Behold the Lamb of God!

37 And the two disciples heard him speak, and they followed Jesus.

38 Then Jesus turned, and saw them following, and saith unto them, What seek ye? They said unto him, Rabbi, (which is to say, being interpreted, Master,) where dwellest thou?

39 He saith unto them, Come and see. They came and saw where he dwelt, and abode with him that day: for it was about the tenth hour.

40 One of the two which heard John *speak*, and followed him, was Andrew, Simon Peter's brother.

41 He first findeth his own brother Simon, and saith unto him, We have found the Messias, which is, being interpreted, the Christ.

42 And he brought him to Jesus. And when Jesus beheld him, he said, Thou art Simon the son of Jona: thou shalt be called Cephas, which is by interpretation, A stone.

43 ¶ The day following Jesus would go forth into Galilee, and findeth Philip, and saith unto him, Follow me.

44 Now Philip was of Bethsaida, the city of Andrew and Peter.

45 Philip findeth Nathanael, and saith unto him, We have found him, of whom Moses in the law, and the prophets, did write, Jesus of Nazareth, the son of Joseph.

46 And Nathanael said unto him, Can there any good thing come out of Nazareth? Philip saith unto him, Come and see.

47 Jesus saw Nathanael coming to him, and saith of him, Behold an Israelite indeed, in whom is no guile!

48 Nathanael saith unto him, Whence knowest thou me? Jesus answered and said unto him, Before that Philip called thee, when thou wast under the fig tree, I saw thee.

49 Nathanael answered and saith unto him, Rabbi, thou art the Son of God; thou art the King of Israel.

50 Jesus answered and said unto him, Because I said unto thee, I saw thee under the fig tree, believest thou? thou shalt see greater things than these.

51 And he saith unto him, Verily, verily, I say unto you, Hereafter ye shall see heaven open, and the angels of God ascending and descending upon the Son of man.

CHAPTER 2

AND the third day there was a marriage in Cana of Galilee; and the mother of Jesus was there:

2 And both Jesus was called, and his disciples, to the marriage.

3 And when they wanted wine, the mother of Jesus saith unto him, They have no wine.

4 Jesus saith unto her, Woman, what have I to do with thee? mine hour is not yet come.

5 His mother saith unto the servants, Whatsoever he saith unto you, do *it*.

6 And there were set there six waterpots of stone, after the manner of the purifying of the Jews, containing two or three firkins apiece.

7 Jesus saith unto them, Fill the waterpots with water. And they filled them up to the brim.

8 And he saith unto them, Draw out now, and bear unto the governor of the feast. And they bare *it*.

9 When the ruler of the feast had tasted the water that was made wine, and knew not whence it was: (but the servants which drew the water knew;) the governor of the feast called the bridegroom,

10 And saith unto him, Every man at the beginning doth set forth good wine; and when men have well drunk, then that which is worse: *but* thou hast kept the good wine until now.

11 This beginning of miracles did Jesus in Cana of Galilee, and manifested forth his glory; and his disciples believed on him.

12 ¶ After this he went down to Capernaum, he, and his mother, and his brethren, and his disciples: and they continued there not many days.

13 ¶ And the Jews' passover was at hand, and Jesus went up to Jerusalem,

14 And found in the temple those that sold oxen and sheep and doves, and the changers of money sitting:

15 And when he had made a scourge of small cords, he drove them all out of the temple, and the sheep, and the oxen; and poured out the changers' money, and overthrew the tables;

16 And said unto them that sold doves, Take these things hence; make not my Father's house an house of merchandise.

17 And his disciples remem-

bered that it was written, The zeal of thine house hath eaten me up.

18 ¶ Then answered the Jews and said unto him, What sign shewest thou unto us, seeing that thou doest these things?

19 Jesus answered and said unto them, Destroy this temple, and in three days I will raise it up.

20 Then said the Jews, Forty and six years was this temple in building, and wilt thou rear it up in three days?

21 But he spake of the temple of his body.

22 When therefore he was risen from the dead, his disciples remembered that he had said this unto them; and they believed the scripture, and the word which Jesus had said.

23 ¶ Now when he was in Jerusalem at the passover, in the feast *day*, many believed in his name, when they saw the miracles which he did.

24 But Jesus did not commit himself unto them, because he knew all *men*,

25 And needed not that any should testify of man: for he knew what was in man.

CHAPTER 3

THERE was a man of the Pharisees, named Nicodemus, a ruler of the Jews:

2 The same came to Jesus by night, and said unto him, Rabbi, we know that thou art a teacher come from God: for no man can do these miracles that thou doest, except God be with him.

3 Jesus answered and said unto him, Verily, verily, I say unto thee, Except a man be born again, he cannot see the kingdom of God.

4 Nicodemus saith unto him, How can a man be born when he is old? can he enter the second time into his mother's womb, and be born?

5 Jesus answered, Verily, verily, I say unto thee, Except a man be born of water and *of* the Spirit, he cannot enter into the kingdom of God.

6 That which is born of the flesh is flesh; and that which is born of the Spirit is spirit.

7 Marvel not that I said unto thee, Ye must be born again.

8 The wind bloweth where it listeth, and thou hearest the sound thereof, but canst not tell whence it cometh, and whither it goeth: so is every one that is born of the Spirit.

9 Nicodemus answered and said unto him, How can these things be?

10 Jesus answered and said unto him, Art thou a master of Israel, and knowest not these things?

11 Verily, verily, I say unto thee, We speak that we do know, and testify that we have seen; and ye receive not our witness.

12 If I have told you earthly things, and ye believe not, how shall ye believe, if I tell you *of* heavenly things?

13 And no man hath ascended up to heaven, but he that came down from heaven, *even* the Son of man which is in heaven.

14 ¶ And as Moses lifted up the serpent in the wilderness, even so

must the Son of man be lifted up:

15 That whosoever believeth in him should not perish, but have eternal life.

16 ¶ For God so loved the world, that he gave his only begotten Son, that whosoever believeth in him should not perish, but have everlasting life.

17 For God sent not his Son into the world to condemn the world; but that the world through him might be saved.

18 ¶ He that believeth on him is not condemned: but he that believeth not is condemned already, because he hath not believed in the name of the only begotten Son of God.

19 And this is the condemnation, that light is come into the world, and men loved darkness rather than light, because their deeds were evil.

20 For every one that doeth evil hateth the light, neither cometh to the light, lest his deeds should be reproved.

21 But he that doeth truth cometh to the light, that his deeds may be made manifest, that they are wrought in God.

22 ¶ After these things came Jesus and his disciples into the land of Judaea; and there he tarried with them, and baptized.

23 ¶ And John also was baptizing in Aenon near to Salim, because there was much water there: and they came, and were baptized.

24 For John was not yet cast into prison.

25 ¶ Then there arose a question between *some* of John's disciples and the Jews about purifying.

26 And they came unto John, and said unto him, Rabbi, he that was with thee beyond Jordan, to whom thou barest witness, behold, the same baptizeth, and all *men* come to him.

27 John answered and said, A man can receive nothing, except it be given him from heaven.

28 Ye yourselves bear me witness, that I said, I am not the Christ, but that I am sent before him.

29 He that hath the bride is the bridegroom: but the friend of the bridegroom, which standeth and heareth him, rejoiceth greatly because of the bridegroom's voice: this my joy therefore is fulfilled.

30 He must increase, but I *must* decrease.

31 He that cometh from above is above all: he that is of the earth is earthly, and speaketh of the earth: he that cometh from heaven is above all.

32 And what he hath seen and heard, that he testifieth; and no man receiveth his testimony.

33 He that hath received his testimony hath set to his seal that God is true.

34 For he whom God hath sent speaketh the words of God: for God giveth not the Spirit by measure *unto him*.

35 The Father loveth the Son, and hath given all things into his hand.

36 He that believeth on the Son hath everlasting life: and he that believeth not the Son shall not see life; but the wrath of God abideth on him.

CHAPTER 4

WHEN therefore the Lord knew how the Pharisees had heard that Jesus made and baptized more disciples than John,

2 (Though Jesus himself baptized not, but his disciples,)

3 He left Judaea, and departed again into Galilee.

4 And he must needs go through Samaria.

5 Then cometh he to a city of Samaria, which is called Sychar, near to the parcel of ground that Jacob gave to his son Joseph.

6 Now Jacob's well was there. Jesus therefore, being wearied with *his* journey, sat thus on the well: *and* it was about the sixth hour.

7 There cometh a woman of Samaria to draw water: Jesus saith unto her, Give me to drink.

8 (For his disciples were gone away unto the city to buy meat.)

9 Then saith the woman of Samaria unto him, How is it that thou, being a Jew, askest drink of me, which am a woman of Samaria? for the Jews have no dealings with the Samaritans.

10 Jesus answered and said unto her, If thou knewest the gift of God, and who it is that saith to thee, Give me to drink; thou wouldest have asked of him, and he would have given thee living water.

11 The woman saith unto him, Sir, thou hast nothing to draw with, and the well is deep: from whence then hast thou that living water?

12 Art thou greater than our father Jacob, which gave us the well, and drank thereof himself, and his children, and his cattle?

13 Jesus answered and said unto her, Whosoever drinketh of this water shall thirst again:

14 But whosoever drinketh of the water that I shall give him shall never thirst; but the water that I shall give him shall be in him a well of water springing up into everlasting life.

15 The woman saith unto him, Sir, give me this water, that I thirst not, neither come hither to draw.

16 Jesus saith unto her, Go, call thy husband, and come hither.

17 The woman answered and said, I have no husband. Jesus said unto her, Thou hast well said, I have no husband:

18 For thou hast had five husbands; and he whom thou now hast is not thy husband: in that saidst thou truly.

19 The woman saith unto him, Sir, I perceive that thou art a prophet.

20 Our fathers worshipped in this mountain; and ye say, that in Jerusalem is the place where men ought to worship.

21 Jesus saith unto her, Woman, believe me, the hour cometh, when ye shall neither in this mountain, nor yet at Jerusalem, worship the Father.

22 Ye worship ye know not what: we know what we worship: for salvation is of the Jews.

23 But the hour cometh, and now is, when the true worshippers shall worship the Father in spirit and in truth: for the Father seeketh such to worship him.

24 God *is* a Spirit: and they that worship him must worship *him* in spirit and in truth.

25 The woman saith unto him, I know that Messias cometh, which is called Christ: when he is come, he will tell us all things.

26 Jesus saith unto her, I that speak unto thee am *he.*

27 ¶ And upon this came his disciples, and marvelled that he talked with the woman: yet no man said, What seekest thou? or, Why talkest thou with her?

28 The woman then left her waterpot, and went her way into the city, and saith to the men,

29 Come, see a man, which told me all things that ever I did: is not this the Christ?

30 Then they went out of the city, and came unto him.

31 ¶ In the mean while his disciples prayed him, saying, Master, eat.

32 But he said unto them, I have meat to eat that ye know not of.

33 Therefore said the disciples one to another, Hath any man brought him *ought* to eat?

34 Jesus saith unto them, My meat is to do the will of him that sent me, and to finish his work.

35 Say not ye, There are yet four months, and *then* cometh harvest? behold, I say unto you, Lift up your eyes, and look on the fields; for they are white already to harvest.

36 And he that reapeth receiveth wages, and gathereth fruit unto life eternal: that both he that soweth and he that reapeth may rejoice together.

37 And herein is that saying true, One soweth, and another reapeth.

38 I sent you to reap that whereon ye bestowed no labour: other men laboured, and ye are entered into their labours.

39 ¶ And many of the Samaritans of that city believed on him for the saying of the woman, which testified, He told me all that ever I did.

40 So when the Samaritans were come unto him, they besought him that he would tarry with them: and he abode there two days.

41 And many more believed because of his own word;

42 And said unto the woman, Now we believe, not because of thy saying: for we have heard *him* ourselves, and know that this is indeed the Christ, the Saviour of the world.

43 ¶ Now after two days he departed thence, and went into Galilee.

44 For Jesus himself testified, that a prophet hath no honour in his own country.

45 Then when he was come into Galilee, the Galilaeans received him, having seen all the things that he did at Jerusalem at the feast: for they also went unto the feast.

46 So Jesus came again into Cana of Galilee, where he made the water wine. And there was a certain nobleman, whose son was sick at Capernaum.

47 When he heard that Jesus was come out of Judaea into Galilee, he went unto him, and besought him that he would come down, and heal his son: for he was at the point of death.

48 Then said Jesus unto him, Except ye see signs and wonders, ye will not believe.

49 The nobleman saith unto him, Sir, come down ere my child die.

50 Jesus saith unto him, Go thy way; thy son liveth. And the man believed the word that Jesus had spoken unto him, and he went his way.

51 And as he was now going down, his servants met him, and told *him*, saying, Thy son liveth.

52 Then enquired he of them the hour when he began to amend. And they said unto him, Yesterday at the seventh hour the fever left him.

53 So the father knew that *it was* at the same hour, in the which Jesus said unto him, Thy son liveth: and himself believed, and his whole house.

54 This *is* again the second miracle *that* Jesus did, when he was come out of Judaea into Galilee.

CHAPTER 5

AFTER this there was a feast of the Jews; and Jesus went up to Jerusalem.

2 Now there is at Jerusalem by the sheep *market* a pool, which is called in the Hebrew tongue Bethesda, having five porches.

3 In these lay a great multitude of impotent folk, of blind, halt, withered, waiting for the moving of the water.

4 For an angel went down at a certain season into the pool, and troubled the water: whosoever then first after the troubling of the water stepped in was made whole of whatsoever disease he had.

5 And a certain man was there, which had an infirmity thirty and eight years.

6 When Jesus saw him lie, and knew that he had been now a long time *in that case*, he saith unto him, Wilt thou be made whole?

7 The impotent man answered him, Sir, I have no man, when the water is troubled, to put me into the pool: but while I am coming, another steppeth down before me.

8 Jesus saith unto him, Rise, take up thy bed, and walk.

9 And immediately the man was made whole, and took up his bed, and walked: and on the same day was the sabbath.

10 ¶ The Jews therefore said unto him that was cured, It is the sabbath day: it is not lawful for thee to carry *thy* bed.

11 He answered them, He that made me whole, the same said unto me, Take up thy bed, and walk.

12 Then asked they him, What man is that which said unto thee, Take up thy bed, and walk?

13 And he that was healed wist not who it was: for Jesus had conveyed himself away, a multitude being in *that* place.

14 Afterward Jesus findeth him in the temple, and said unto him, Behold, thou art made whole: sin no more, lest a worse thing come unto thee.

15 The man departed, and told the Jews that it was Jesus, which had made him whole.

16 And therefore did the Jews persecute Jesus, and sought to slay him, because he had done these things on the sabbath day.

17 ¶ But Jesus answered them, My Father worketh hitherto, and I work.

18 Therefore the Jews sought the more to kill him, because he not only had broken the sabbath, but said also that God was his Father, making himself equal with God.

19 Then answered Jesus and said unto them, Verily, verily, I say unto you, The Son can do nothing of himself, but what he seeth the Father do: for what things soever he doeth, these also doeth the Son likewise.

20 For the Father loveth the Son, and sheweth him all things that himself doeth: and he will shew him greater works than these, that ye may marvel.

21 For as the Father raiseth up the dead, and quickeneth *them*; even so the Son quickeneth whom he will.

22 For the Father judgeth no man, but hath committed all judgment unto the Son:

23 That all *men* should honour the Son, even as they honour the Father. He that honoureth not the Son honoureth not the Father which hath sent him.

24 Verily, verily, I say unto you, He that heareth my word, and believeth on him that sent me, hath everlasting life, and shall not come into condemnation; but is passed from death unto life.

25 Verily, verily, I say unto you, The hour is coming, and now is, when the dead shall hear the voice of the Son of God: and they that hear shall live.

26 For as the Father hath life in himself; so hath he given to the Son to have life in himself;

27 And hath given him authority to execute judgment also, because he is the Son of man.

28 Marvel not at this: for the hour is coming, in the which all that are in the graves shall hear his voice,

29 And shall come forth; they that have done good, unto the resurrection of life; and they that have done evil, unto the resurrection of damnation.

30 I can of mine own self do nothing: as I hear, I judge: and my judgment is just; because I seek not mine own will, but the will of the Father which hath sent me.

31 If I bear witness of myself, my witness is not true.

32 ¶ There is another that beareth witness of me; and I know that the witness which he witnesseth of me is true.

33 Ye sent unto John, and he bare witness unto the truth.

34 But I receive not testimony from man: but these things I say, that ye might be saved.

35 He was a burning and a shining light: and ye were willing for a season to rejoice in his light.

36 ¶ But I have greater witness than *that* of John: for the works which the Father hath given me to finish, the same works that I do, bear witness of me, that the Father hath sent me.

37 And the Father himself,

which hath sent me, hath borne witness of me. Ye have neither heard his voice at any time, nor seen his shape.

38 And ye have not his word abiding in you: for whom he hath sent, him ye believe not.

39 ¶ Search the scriptures; for in them ye think ye have eternal life: and they are they which testify of me.

40 And ye will not come to me, that ye might have life.

41 I receive not honour from men.

42 But I know you, that ye have not the love of God in you.

43 I am come in my Father's name, and ye receive me not: if another shall come in his own name, him ye will receive.

44 How can ye believe, which receive honour one of another, and seek not the honour that *cometh* from God only?

45 Do not think that I will accuse you to the Father: there is *one* that accuseth you, *even* Moses, in whom ye trust.

46 For had ye believed Moses, ye would have believed me: for he wrote of me.

47 But if ye believe not his writings, how shall ye believe my words?

CHAPTER 6

AFTER these things Jesus went over the sea of Galilee, which is *the sea* of Tiberias.

2 And a great multitude followed him, because they saw his miracles which he did on them that were diseased.

3 And Jesus went up into a mountain, and there he sat with his disciples.

4 And the passover, a feast of the Jews, was nigh.

5 ¶ When Jesus then lifted up *his* eyes, and saw a great company come unto him, he saith unto Philip, Whence shall we buy bread, that these may eat?

6 And this he said to prove him: for he himself knew what he would do.

7 Philip answered him, Two hundred pennyworth of bread is not sufficient for them, that every one of them may take a little.

8 One of his disciples, Andrew, Simon Peter's brother, saith unto him,

9 There is a lad here, which hath five barley loaves, and two small fishes: but what are they among so many?

10 And Jesus said, Make the men sit down. Now there was much grass in the place. So the men sat down, in number about five thousand.

11 And Jesus took the loaves; and when he had given thanks, he distributed to the disciples, and the disciples to them that were set down; and likewise of the fishes as much as they would.

12 When they were filled, he said unto his disciples, Gather up the fragments that remain, that nothing be lost.

13 Therefore they gathered *them* together, and filled twelve baskets with the fragments of the five barley loaves, which remained over and above unto them that had eaten.

14 Then those men, when they

had seen the miracle that Jesus did, said, This is of a truth that prophet that should come into the world.

15 ¶ When Jesus therefore perceived that they would come and take him by force, to make him a king, he departed again into a mountain himself alone.

16 And when even was *now* come, his disciples went down unto the sea,

17 And entered into a ship, and went over the sea toward Capernaum. And it was now dark, and Jesus was not come to them.

18 And the sea arose by reason of a great wind that blew.

19 So when they had rowed about five and twenty or thirty furlongs, they see Jesus walking on the sea, and drawing nigh unto the ship: and they were afraid.

20 But he saith unto them, It is I; be not afraid.

21 Then they willingly received him into the ship: and immediately the ship was at the land whither they went.

22 ¶ The day following, when the people which stood on the other side of the sea saw that there was none other boat there, save that one whereinto his disciples were entered, and that Jesus went not with his disciples into the boat, but *that* his disciples were gone away alone;

23 (Howbeit there came other boats from Tiberias nigh unto the place where they did eat bread, after that the Lord had given thanks:)

24 When the people therefore saw that Jesus was not there, nei-ther his disciples, they also took shipping, and came to Capernaum, seeking for Jesus.

25 And when they had found him on the other side of the sea, they said unto him, Rabbi, when camest thou hither?

26 Jesus answered them and said, Verily, verily, I say unto you, Ye seek me, not because ye saw the miracles, but because ye did eat of the loaves, and were filled.

27 Labour not for the meat which perisheth, but for that meat which endureth unto everlasting life, which the Son of man shall give unto you: for him hath God the Father sealed.

28 Then said they unto him, What shall we do, that we might work the works of God?

29 Jesus answered and said unto them, This is the work of God, that ye believe on him whom he hath sent.

30 They said therefore unto him, What sign shewest thou then, that we may see, and believe thee? what dost thou work?

31 Our fathers did eat manna in the desert; as it is written, He gave them bread from heaven to eat.

32 Then Jesus said unto them, Verily, verily, I say unto you, Moses gave you not that bread from heaven; but my Father giveth you the true bread from heaven.

33 For the bread of God is he which cometh down from heaven, and giveth life unto the world.

34 Then said they unto him, Lord, evermore give us this bread.

35 And Jesus said unto them, I am the bread of life: he that cometh to me shall never hunger; and he that believeth on me shall never thirst.

36 But I said unto you, That ye also have seen me, and believe not.

37 All that the Father giveth me shall come to me; and him that cometh to me I will in no wise cast out.

38 For I came down from heaven, not to do mine own will, but the will of him that sent me.

39 And this is the Father's will which hath sent me, that of all which he hath given me I should lose nothing, but should raise it up again at the last day.

40 And this is the will of him that sent me, that every one which seeth the Son, and believeth on him, may have everlasting life: and I will raise him up at the last day.

41 The Jews then murmured at him, because he said, I am the bread which came down from heaven.

42 And they said, Is not this Jesus, the son of Joseph, whose father and mother we know? how is it then that he saith, I came down from heaven?

43 Jesus therefore answered and said unto them, Murmur not among yourselves.

44 No man can come to me, except the Father which hath sent me draw him: and I will raise him up at the last day.

45 It is written in the prophets, And they shall be all taught of God. Every man therefore that hath heard, and hath learned of the Father, cometh unto me.

46 Not that any man hath seen the Father, save he which is of God, he hath seen the Father.

47 Verily, verily, I say unto you, He that believeth on me hath everlasting life.

48 I am that bread of life.

49 Your fathers did eat manna in the wilderness, and are dead.

50 This is the bread which cometh down from heaven, that a man may eat thereof, and not die.

51 I am the living bread which came down from heaven: if any man eat of this bread, he shall live for ever: and the bread that I will give is my flesh, which I will give for the life of the world.

52 The Jews therefore strove among themselves, saying, How can this man give us his flesh to eat?

53 Then Jesus said unto them, Verily, verily, I say unto you, Except ye eat the flesh of the Son of man, and drink his blood, ye have no life in you.

54 Whoso eateth my flesh, and drinketh my blood, hath eternal life; and I will raise him up at the last day.

55 For my flesh is meat indeed, and my blood is drink indeed.

56 He that eateth my flesh, and drinketh my blood, dwelleth in me, and I in him.

57 As the living Father hath sent me, and I live by the Father: so he that eateth me, even he shall live by me.

58 This is that bread which came down from heaven: not as

your fathers did eat manna, and are dead: he that eateth of this bread shall live for ever.

59 These things said he in the synagogue, as he taught in Capernaum.

60 Many therefore of his disciples, when they had heard *this*, said, This is an hard saying; who can hear it?

61 When Jesus knew in himself that his disciples murmured at it, he said unto them, Doth this offend you?

62 *What* and if ye shall see the Son of man ascend up where he was before?

63 It is the spirit that quickeneth; the flesh profiteth nothing: the words that I speak unto you, *they* are spirit, and *they* are life.

64 But there are some of you that believe not. For Jesus knew from the beginning who they were that believed not, and who should betray him.

65 And he said, Therefore said I unto you, that no man can come unto me, except it were given unto him of my Father.

66 ¶ From that *time* many of his disciples went back, and walked no more with him.

67 Then said Jesus unto the twelve, Will ye also go away?

68 Then Simon Peter answered him, Lord, to whom shall we go? thou hast the words of eternal life.

69 And we believe and are sure that thou art that Christ, the Son of the living God.

70 Jesus answered them, Have not I chosen you twelve, and one of you is a devil?

71 He spake of Judas Iscariot *the son* of Simon: for he it was that should betray him, being one of the twelve.

CHAPTER 7

AFTER these things Jesus walked in Galilee: for he would not walk in Jewry, because the Jews sought to kill him.

2 Now the Jews' feast of tabernacles was at hand.

3 His brethren therefore said unto him, Depart hence, and go into Judaea, that thy disciples also may see the works that thou doest.

4 For *there is* no man *that* doeth any thing in secret, and he himself seeketh to be known openly. If thou do these things, shew thyself to the world.

5 For neither did his brethren believe in him.

6 Then Jesus said unto them, My time is not yet come: but your time is alway ready.

7 The world cannot hate you; but me it hateth, because I testify of it, that the works thereof are evil.

8 Go ye up unto this feast: I go not up yet unto this feast; for my time is not yet full come.

9 When he had said these words unto them, he abode *still* in Galilee.

10 ¶ But when his brethren were gone up, then went he also up unto the feast, not openly, but as it were in secret.

11 Then the Jews sought him at the feast, and said, Where is he?

12 And there was much murmuring among the people con-

cerning him: for some said, He is a good man: others said, Nay; but he deceiveth the people.

13 Howbeit no man spake openly of him for fear of the Jews.

14 ¶ Now about the midst of the feast Jesus went up into the temple, and taught.

15 And the Jews marvelled, saying, How knoweth this man letters, having never learned?

16 Jesus answered them, and said, My doctrine is not mine, but his that sent me.

17 If any man will do his will, he shall know of the doctrine, whether it be of God, or *whether* I speak of myself.

18 He that speaketh of himself seeketh his own glory: but he that seeketh his glory that sent him, the same is true, and no unrighteousness is in him.

19 Did not Moses give you the law, and *yet* none of you keepeth the law? Why go ye about to kill me?

20 The people answered and said, Thou hast a devil: who goeth about to kill thee?

21 Jesus answered and said unto them, I have done one work, and ye all marvel.

22 Moses therefore gave unto you circumcision; (not because it is of Moses, but of the fathers;) and ye on the sabbath day circumcise a man.

23 If a man on the sabbath day receive circumcision, that the law of Moses should not be broken; are ye angry at me, because I have made a man every whit whole on the sabbath day?

24 Judge not according to the appearance, but judge righteous judgment.

25 Then said some of them of Jerusalem, Is not this he, whom they seek to kill?

26 But, lo, he speaketh boldly, and they say nothing unto him. Do the rulers know indeed that this is the very Christ?

27 Howbeit we know this man whence he is: but when Christ cometh, no man knoweth whence he is.

28 Then cried Jesus in the temple as he taught, saying, Ye both know me, and ye know whence I am: and I am not come of myself, but he that sent me is true, whom ye know not.

29 But I know him: for I am from him, and he hath sent me.

30 Then they sought to take him: but no man laid hands on him, because his hour was not yet come.

31 And many of the people believed on him, and said, When Christ cometh, will he do more miracles than these which this *man* hath done?

32 ¶ The Pharisees heard that the people murmured such things concerning him; and the Pharisees and the chief priests sent officers to take him.

33 Then said Jesus unto them, Yet a little while am I with you, and *then* I go unto him that sent me.

34 Ye shall seek me, and shall not find *me*: and where I am, *thither* ye cannot come.

35 Then said the Jews among themselves, Whither will he go,

that we shall not find him? will he go unto the dispersed among the Gentiles, and teach the Gentiles?

36 What *manner of* saying is this that he said, Ye shall seek me, and shall not find *me*: and where I am, *thither* ye cannot come?

37 In the last day, that great *day* of the feast, Jesus stood and cried, saying, If any man thirst, let him come unto me, and drink.

38 He that believeth on me, as the scripture hath said, out of his belly shall flow rivers of living water.

39 (But this spake he of the Spirit, which they that believe on him should receive: for the Holy Ghost was not yet *given*; because that Jesus was not yet glorified.)

40 ¶ Many of the people therefore, when they heard this saying, said, Of a truth this is the Prophet.

41 Others said, This is the Christ. But some said, Shall Christ come out of Galilee?

42 Hath not the scripture said, That Christ cometh of the seed of David, and out of the town of Bethlehem, where David was?

43 So there was a division among the people because of him.

44 And some of them would have taken him; but no man laid hands on him.

45 ¶ Then came the officers to the chief priests and Pharisees; and they said unto them, Why have ye not brought him?

46 The officers answered, Never man spake like this man.

47 Then answered them the Pharisees, Are ye also deceived?

48 Have any of the rulers or of the Pharisees believed on him?

49 But this people who knoweth not the law are cursed.

50 Nicodemus saith unto them, (he that came to Jesus by night, being one of them,)

51 Doth our law judge *any* man, before it hear him, and know what he doeth?

52 They answered and said unto him, Art thou also of Galilee? Search, and look: for out of Galilee ariseth no prophet.

53 And every man went unto his own house.

CHAPTER 8

JESUS went unto the mount of Olives.

2 And early in the morning he came again into the temple, and all the people came unto him; and he sat down, and taught them.

3 And the scribes and Pharisees brought unto him a woman taken in adultery; and when they had set her in the midst,

4 They say unto him, Master, this woman was taken in adultery, in the very act.

5 Now Moses in the law commanded us, that such should be stoned: but what sayest thou?

6 This they said, tempting him, that they might have to accuse him. But Jesus stooped down, and with *his* finger wrote on the ground, *as though he heard them not.*

7 So when they continued asking him, he lifted up himself, and said unto them, He that is without sin among you, let him first cast a stone at her.

8 And again he stooped down, and wrote on the ground.

9 And they which heard *it*, being convicted by *their own* conscience, went out one by one, beginning at the eldest, *even* unto the last: and Jesus was left alone, and the woman standing in the midst.

10 When Jesus had lifted up himself, and saw none but the woman, he said unto her, Woman, where are those thine accusers? hath no man condemned thee?

11 She said, No man, Lord. And Jesus said unto her, Neither do I condemn thee: go, and sin no more.

12 ¶ Then spake Jesus again unto them, saying, I am the light of the world: he that followeth me shall not walk in darkness, but shall have the light of life.

13 The Pharisees therefore said unto him, Thou bearest record of thyself; thy record is not true.

14 Jesus answered and said unto them, Though I bear record of myself, *yet* my record is true: for I know whence I came, and whither I go; but ye cannot tell whence I come, and whither I go.

15 Ye judge after the flesh; I judge no man.

16 And yet if I judge, my judgment is true: for I am not alone, but I and the Father that sent me.

17 It is also written in your law, that the testimony of two men is true.

18 I am one that bear witness of myself, and the Father that sent me beareth witness of me.

19 Then said they unto him, Where is thy Father? Jesus answered, Ye neither know me, nor my Father: if ye had known me, ye should have known my Father also.

20 These words spake Jesus in the treasury, as he taught in the temple: and no man laid hands on him; for his hour was not yet come.

21 Then said Jesus again unto them, I go my way, and ye shall seek me, and shall die in your sins: whither I go, ye cannot come.

22 Then said the Jews, Will he kill himself? because he saith, Whither I go, ye cannot come.

23 And he said unto them, Ye are from beneath; I am from above: ye are of this world; I am not of this world.

24 I said therefore unto you, that ye shall die in your sins: for if ye believe not that I am *he*, ye shall die in your sins.

25 Then said they unto him, Who art thou? And Jesus saith unto them, Even *the same* that I said unto you from the beginning.

26 I have many things to say and to judge of you: but he that sent me is true; and I speak to the world those things which I have heard of him.

27 They understood not that he spake to them of the Father.

28 Then said Jesus unto them, When ye have lifted up the Son of man, then shall ye know that I am *he*, and *that* I do nothing of myself; but as my Father hath taught me, I speak these things.

29 And he that sent me is with me: the Father hath not left me alone; for I do always those things that please him.

30 As he spake these words, many believed on him.

31 Then said Jesus to those Jews which believed on him, If ye continue in my word, *then* are ye my disciples indeed;

32 And ye shall know the truth, and the truth shall make you free.

33 ¶ They answered him, We be Abraham's seed, and were never in bondage to any man: how sayest thou, Ye shall be made free?

34 Jesus answered them, Verily, verily, I say unto you, Whosoever committeth sin is the servant of sin.

35 And the servant abideth not in the house for ever: *but* the Son abideth ever.

36 If the Son therefore shall make you free, ye shall be free indeed.

37 I know that ye are Abraham's seed; but ye seek to kill me, because my word hath no place in you.

38 I speak that which I have seen with my Father: and ye do that which ye have seen with your father.

39 They answered and said unto him, Abraham is our father. Jesus saith unto them, If ye were Abraham's children, ye would do the works of Abraham.

40 But now ye seek to kill me, a man that hath told you the truth, which I have heard of God: this did not Abraham.

41 Ye do the deeds of your father. Then said they to him, We be not born of fornication; we have one Father, *even* God.

42 Jesus said unto them, If God were your Father, ye would love me: for I proceeded forth and came from God; neither came I of myself, but he sent me.

43 Why do ye not understand my speech? *even* because ye cannot hear my word.

44 Ye are of *your* father the devil, and the lusts of your father ye will do. He was a murderer from the beginning, and abode not in the truth, because there is no truth in him. When he speaketh a lie, he speaketh of his own: for he is a liar, and the father of it.

45 And because I tell *you* the truth, ye believe me not.

46 Which of you convinceth me of sin? And if I say the truth, why do ye not believe me?

47 He that is of God heareth God's words: ye therefore hear *them* not, because ye are not of God.

48 Then answered the Jews, and said unto him, Say we not well that thou art a Samaritan, and hast a devil?

49 Jesus answered, I have not a devil; but I honour my Father, and ye do dishonour me.

50 And I seek not mine own glory: there is one that seeketh and judgeth.

51 Verily, verily, I say unto you, If a man keep my saying, he shall never see death.

52 Then said the Jews unto him, Now we know that thou hast a devil. Abraham is dead, and the prophets; and thou sayest, If a

man keep my saying, he shall never taste of death.

53 Art thou greater than our father Abraham, which is dead? and the prophets are dead: whom makest thou thyself?

54 Jesus answered, If I honour myself, my honour is nothing: it is my Father that honoureth me; of whom ye say, that he is your God:

55 Yet ye have not known him; but I know him: and if I should say, I know him not, I shall be a liar like unto you: but I know him, and keep his saying.

56 Your father Abraham rejoiced to see my day: and he saw *it*, and was glad.

57 Then said the Jews unto him, Thou art not yet fifty years old, and hast thou seen Abraham?

58 Jesus said unto them, Verily, verily, I say unto you, Before Abraham was, I am.

59 Then took they up stones to cast at him: but Jesus hid himself, and went out of the temple, going through the midst of them, and so passed by.

CHAPTER 9

AND as *Jesus* passed by, he saw a man which was blind from *his* birth.

2 And his disciples asked him, saying, Master, who did sin, this man, or his parents, that he was born blind?

3 Jesus answered, Neither hath this man sinned, nor his parents: but that the works of God should be made manifest in him.

4 I must work the works of him that sent me, while it is day: the night cometh, when no man can work.

5 As long as I am in the world, I am the light of the world.

6 When he had thus spoken, he spat on the ground, and made clay of the spittle, and he anointed the eyes of the blind man with the clay,

7 And said unto him, Go, wash in the pool of Siloam, (which is by interpretation, Sent.) He went his way therefore, and washed, and came seeing.

8 ¶ The neighbours therefore, and they which before had seen him that he was blind, said, Is not this he that sat and begged?

9 Some said, This is he: others *said*, He is like him: *but* he said, I am *he*.

10 Therefore said they unto him, How were thine eyes opened?

11 He answered and said, A man that is called Jesus made clay, and anointed mine eyes, and said unto me, Go to the pool of Siloam, and wash: and I went and washed, and I received sight.

12 Then said they unto him, Where is he? He said, I know not.

13 ¶ They brought to the Pharisees him that aforetime was blind.

14 And it was the sabbath day when Jesus made the clay, and opened his eyes.

15 Then again the Pharisees also asked him how he had received his sight. He said unto them, He put clay upon mine eyes, and I washed, and do see.

16 Therefore said some of the Pharisees, This man is not of

God, because he keepeth not the sabbath day. Others said, How can a man that is a sinner do such miracles? And there was a division among them.

17 They say unto the blind man again, What sayest thou of him, that he hath opened thine eyes? He said, He is a prophet.

18 But the Jews did not believe concerning him, that he had been blind, and received his sight, until they called the parents of him that had received his sight.

19 And they asked them, saying, Is this your son, who ye say was born blind? how then doth he now see?

20 His parents answered them and said, We know that this is our son, and that he was born blind:

21 But by what means he now seeth, we know not; or who hath opened his eyes, we know not: he is of age; ask him: he shall speak for himself.

22 These *words* spake his parents, because they feared the Jews: for the Jews had agreed already, that if any man did confess that he was Christ, he should be put out of the synagogue.

23 Therefore said his parents, He is of age; ask him.

24 Then again called they the man that was blind, and said unto him, Give God the praise: we know that this man is a sinner.

25 He answered and said, Whether he be a sinner *or no*, I know not: one thing I know, that, whereas I was blind, now I see.

26 Then said they to him again, What did he to thee? how opened he thine eyes?

27 He answered them, I have told you already, and ye did not hear: wherefore would ye hear *it* again? will ye also be his disciples?

28 Then they reviled him, and said, Thou art his disciple; but we are Moses' disciples.

29 We know that God spake unto Moses: *as for* this *fellow*, we know not from whence he is.

30 The man answered and said unto them, Why herein is a marvellous thing, that ye know not from whence he is, and *yet* he hath opened mine eyes.

31 Now we know that God heareth not sinners: but if any man be a worshipper of God, and doeth his will, him he heareth.

32 Since the world began was it not heard that any man opened the eyes of one that was born blind.

33 If this man were not of God, he could do nothing.

34 They answered and said unto him, Thou wast altogether born in sins, and dost thou teach us? And they cast him out.

35 Jesus heard that they had cast him out; and when he had found him, he said unto him, Dost thou believe on the Son of God?

36 He answered and said, Who is he, Lord, that I might believe on him?

37 And Jesus said unto him, Thou hast both seen him, and it is he that talketh with thee.

38 And he said, Lord, I believe. And he worshipped him.

39 ¶ And Jesus said, For judg-

ment I am come into this world, that they which see not might see; and that they which see might be made blind.

40 And *some* of the Pharisees which were with him heard these words, and said unto him, Are we blind also?

41 Jesus said unto them, If ye were blind, ye should have no sin: but now ye say, We see; therefore your sin remaineth.

CHAPTER 10

VERILY, verily, I say unto you, He that entereth not by the door into the sheepfold, but climbeth up some other way, the same is a thief and a robber.

2 But he that entereth in by the door is the shepherd of the sheep.

3 To him the porter openeth; and the sheep hear his voice: and he calleth his own sheep by name, and leadeth them out.

4 And when he putteth forth his own sheep, he goeth before them, and the sheep follow him: for they know his voice.

5 And a stranger will they not follow, but will flee from him: for they know not the voice of strangers.

6 This parable spake Jesus unto them: but they understood not what things they were which he spake unto them.

7 Then said Jesus unto them again, Verily, verily, I say unto you, I am the door of the sheep.

8 All that ever came before me are thieves and robbers: but the sheep did not hear them.

9 I am the door: by me if any man enter in, he shall be saved, and shall go in and out, and find pasture.

10 The thief cometh not, but for to steal, and to kill, and to destroy: I am come that they might have life, and that they might have *it* more abundantly.

11 I am the good shepherd: the good shepherd giveth his life for the sheep.

12 But he that is an hireling, and not the shepherd, whose own the sheep are not, seeth the wolf coming, and leaveth the sheep, and fleeth: and the wolf catcheth them, and scattereth the sheep.

13 The hireling fleeth, because he is an hireling, and careth not for the sheep.

14 I am the good shepherd, and know my *sheep*, and am known of mine.

15 As the Father knoweth me, even so know I the Father: and I lay down my life for the sheep.

16 And other sheep I have, which are not of this fold: them also I must bring, and they shall hear my voice; and there shall be one fold, *and* one shepherd.

17 Therefore doth my Father love me, because I lay down my life, that I might take it again.

18 No man taketh it from me, but I lay it down of myself. I have power to lay it down, and I have power to take it again. This commandment have I received of my Father.

19 ¶ There was a division therefore again among the Jews for these sayings.

20 And many of them said, He hath a devil, and is mad; why hear ye him?

21 Others said, These are not the words of him that hath a devil. Can a devil open the eyes of the blind?

22 ¶ And it was at Jerusalem the feast of the dedication, and it was winter.

23 And Jesus walked in the temple in Solomon's porch.

24 Then came the Jews round about him, and said unto him, How long dost thou make us to doubt? If thou be the Christ, tell us plainly.

25 Jesus answered them, I told you, and ye believed not: the works that I do in my Father's name, they bear witness of me.

26 But ye believe not, because ye are not of my sheep, as I said unto you.

27 My sheep hear my voice, and I know them, and they follow me:

28 And I give unto them eternal life; and they shall never perish, neither shall any *man* pluck them out of my hand.

29 My Father, which gave *them* me, is greater than all; and no *man* is able to pluck *them* out of my Father's hand.

30 I and *my* Father are one.

31 Then the Jews took up stones again to stone him.

32 Jesus answered them, Many good works have I shewed you from my Father; for which of those works do ye stone me?

33 The Jews answered him, saying, For a good work we stone thee not; but for blasphemy; and because that thou, being a man, makest thyself God.

34 Jesus answered them, Is it not written in your law, I said, Ye are gods?

35 If he called them gods, unto whom the word of God came, and the scripture cannot be broken;

36 Say ye of him, whom the Father hath sanctified, and sent into the world, Thou blasphemest; because I said, I am the Son of God?

37 If I do not the works of my Father, believe me not.

38 But if I do, though ye believe not me, believe the works: that ye may know, and believe, that the Father *is* in me, and I in him.

39 Therefore they sought again to take him: but he escaped out of their hand,

40 And went away again beyond Jordan into the place where John at first baptized; and there he abode.

41 And many resorted unto him, and said, John did no miracle: but all things that John spake of this man were true.

42 And many believed on him there.

CHAPTER 11

NOW a certain *man* was sick, *named* Lazarus, of Bethany, the town of Mary and her sister Martha.

2 (It was *that* Mary which anointed the Lord with ointment, and wiped his feet with her hair, whose brother Lazarus was sick.)

3 Therefore his sisters sent unto him, saying, Lord, behold, he whom thou lovest is sick.

4 When Jesus heard *that*, he said, This sickness is not unto

death, but for the glory of God, that the Son of God might be glorified thereby.

5 Now Jesus loved Martha, and her sister, and Lazarus.

6 When he had heard therefore that he was sick, he abode two days still in the same place where he was.

7 Then after that saith he to *his* disciples, Let us go into Judaea again.

8 *His* disciples say unto him, Master, the Jews of late sought to stone thee; and goest thou thither again?

9 Jesus answered, Are there not twelve hours in the day? If any man walk in the day, he stumbleth not, because he seeth the light of this world.

10 But if a man walk in the night, he stumbleth, because there is no light in him.

11 These things said he: and after that he saith unto them, Our friend Lazarus sleepeth; but I go, that I may awake him out of sleep.

12 Then said his disciples, Lord, if he sleep, he shall do well.

13 Howbeit Jesus spake of his death: but they thought that he had spoken of taking of rest in sleep.

14 Then said Jesus unto them plainly, Lazarus is dead.

15 And I am glad for your sakes that I was not there, to the intent ye may believe; nevertheless let us go unto him.

16 Then said Thomas, which is called Didymus, unto his fellow-disciples, Let us also go, that we may die with him.

17 Then when Jesus came, he found that he had *lain* in the grave four days already.

18 Now Bethany was nigh unto Jerusalem, about fifteen furlongs off:

19 And many of the Jews came to Martha and Mary, to comfort them concerning their brother.

20 Then Martha, as soon as she heard that Jesus was coming, went and met him: but Mary sat *still* in the house.

21 Then said Martha unto Jesus, Lord, if thou hadst been here, my brother had not died.

22 But I know, that even now, whatsoever thou wilt ask of God, God will give *it* thee.

23 Jesus saith unto her, Thy brother shall rise again.

24 Martha saith unto him, I know that he shall rise again in the resurrection at the last day.

25 Jesus said unto her, I am the resurrection, and the life: he that believeth in me, though he were dead, yet shall he live:

26 And whosoever liveth and believeth in me shall never die. Believest thou this?

27 She saith unto him, Yea, Lord: I believe that thou art the Christ, the Son of God, which should come into the world.

28 And when she had so said, she went her way, and called Mary her sister secretly, saying, The Master is come, and calleth for thee.

29 As soon as she heard *that*, she arose quickly, and came unto him.

30 Now Jesus was not yet come into the town, but was in that place where Martha met him.

31 The Jews then which were with her in the house, and comforted her, when they saw Mary, that she rose up hastily and went out, followed her, saying, She goeth unto the grave to weep there.

32 Then when Mary was come where Jesus was, and saw him, she fell down at his feet, saying unto him, Lord, if thou hadst been here, my brother had not died.

33 When Jesus therefore saw her weeping, and the Jews also weeping which came with her, he groaned in the spirit, and was troubled,

34 And said, Where have ye laid him? They said unto him, Lord, come and see.

35 Jesus wept.

36 Then said the Jews, Behold how he loved him!

37 And some of them said, Could not this man, which opened the eyes of the blind, have caused that even this man should not have died?

38 Jesus therefore again groaning in himself cometh to the grave. It was a cave, and a stone lay upon it.

39 Jesus said, Take ye away the stone. Martha, the sister of him that was dead, saith unto him, Lord, by this time he stinketh: for he hath been *dead* four days.

40 Jesus saith unto her, Said I not unto thee, that, if thou wouldest believe, thou shouldest see the glory of God?

41 Then they took away the stone *from the place* where the dead was laid. And Jesus lifted up *his* eyes, and said, Father, I thank thee that thou hast heard me.

42 And I knew that thou hearest me always: but because of the people which stand by I said *it*, that they may believe that thou hast sent me.

43 And when he thus had spoken, he cried with a loud voice, Lazarus, come forth.

44 And he that was dead came forth, bound hand and foot with graveclothes: and his face was bound about with a napkin. Jesus saith unto them, Loose him, and let him go.

45 Then many of the Jews which came to Mary, and had seen the things which Jesus did, believed on him.

46 But some of them went their ways to the Pharisees, and told them what things Jesus had done.

47 ¶ Then gathered the chief priests and the Pharisees a council, and said, What do we? for this man doeth many miracles.

48 If we let him thus alone, all *men* will believe on him: and the Romans shall come and take away both our place and nation.

49 And one of them, *named* Caiaphas, being the high priest that same year, said unto them, Ye know nothing at all,

50 Nor consider that it is expedient for us, that one man should die for the people, and that the whole nation perish not.

51 And this spake he not of himself: but being high priest that year, he prophesied that Jesus should die for that nation;

52 And not for that nation only, but that also he should gather together in one the children of God that were scattered abroad.

53 Then from that day forth they took counsel together for to put him to death.

54 Jesus therefore walked no more openly among the Jews; but went thence unto a country near to the wilderness, into a city called Ephraim, and there continued with his disciples.

55 ¶ And the Jews' passover was nigh at hand: and many went out of the country up to Jerusalem before the passover, to purify themselves.

56 Then sought they for Jesus, and spake among themselves, as they stood in the temple, What think ye, that he will not come to the feast?

57 Now both the chief priests and the Pharisees had given a commandment, that, if any man knew where he were, he should shew it, that they might take him.

CHAPTER 12

THEN Jesus six days before the passover came to Bethany, where Lazarus was which had been dead, whom he raised from the dead.

2 There they made him a supper; and Martha served: but Lazarus was one of them that sat at the table with him.

3 Then took Mary a pound of ointment of spikenard, very costly, and anointed the feet of Jesus, and wiped his feet with her hair: and the house was filled with the odour of the ointment.

4 Then saith one of his disciples, Judas Iscariot, Simon's son, which should betray him,

5 Why was not this ointment sold for three hundred pence, and given to the poor?

6 This he said, not that he cared for the poor; but because he was a thief, and had the bag, and bare what was put therein.

7 Then said Jesus, Let her alone: against the day of my burying hath she kept this.

8 For the poor always ye have with you; but me ye have not always.

9 Much people of the Jews therefore knew that he was there: and they came not for Jesus' sake only, but that they might see Lazarus also, whom he had raised from the dead.

10 ¶ But the chief priests consulted that they might put Lazarus also to death;

11 Because that by reason of him many of the Jews went away, and believed on Jesus.

12 ¶ On the next day much people that were come to the feast, when they heard that Jesus was coming to Jerusalem,

13 Took branches of palm trees, and went forth to meet him, and cried, Hosanna: Blessed is the King of Israel that cometh in the name of the Lord.

14 And Jesus, when he had found a young ass, sat thereon; as it is written,

15 Fear not, daughter of Sion: behold, thy King cometh, sitting on an ass's colt.

16 These things understood not his disciples at the first: but when

Jesus was glorified, then remembered they that these things were written of him, and *that* they had done these things unto him.

17 The people therefore that was with him when he called Lazarus out of his grave, and raised him from the dead, bare record.

18 For this cause the people also met him, for that they heard that he had done this miracle.

19 The Pharisees therefore said among themselves, Perceive ye how ye prevail nothing? behold, the world is gone after him.

20 ¶ And there were certain Greeks among them that came up to worship at the feast:

21 The same came therefore to Philip, which was of Bethsaida of Galilee, and desired him, saying, Sir, we would see Jesus.

22 Philip cometh and telleth Andrew: and again Andrew and Philip tell Jesus.

23 ¶ And Jesus answered them, saying, The hour is come, that the Son of man should be glorified.

24 Verily, verily, I say unto you, Except a corn of wheat fall into the ground and die, it abideth alone: but if it die, it bringeth forth much fruit.

25 He that loveth his life shall lose it; and he that hateth his life in this world shall keep it unto life eternal.

26 If any man serve me, let him follow me; and where I am, there shall also my servant be: if any man serve me, him will *my* Father honour.

27 Now is my soul troubled; and what shall I say? Father, save me from this hour: but for this cause came I unto this hour.

28 Father, glorify thy name. Then came there a voice from heaven, *saying*, I have both glorified *it*, and will glorify *it* again.

29 The people therefore, that stood by, and heard *it*, said that it thundered: others said, An angel spake to him.

30 Jesus answered and said, This voice came not because of me, but for your sakes.

31 Now is the judgment of this world: now shall the prince of this world be cast out.

32 And I, if I be lifted up from the earth, will draw all *men* unto me.

33 This he said, signifying what death he should die.

34 The people answered him, We have heard out of the law that Christ abideth for ever: and how sayest thou, The Son of man must be lifted up? who is this Son of man?

35 Then Jesus said unto them, Yet a little while is the light with you. Walk while ye have the light, lest darkness come upon you: for he that walketh in darkness knoweth not whither he goeth.

36 While ye have light, believe in the light, that ye may be the children of light. These things spake Jesus, and departed, and did hide himself from them.

37 ¶ But though he had done so many miracles before them, yet they believed not on him:

38 That the saying of Esaias the prophet might be fulfilled, which he spake, Lord, who hath believed our report? and to whom

hath the arm of the Lord been revealed?

39 Therefore they could not believe, because that Esaias said again,

40 He hath blinded their eyes, and hardened their heart; that they should not see with *their* eyes, nor understand with *their* heart, and be converted, and I should heal them.

41 These things said Esaias, when he saw his glory, and spake of him.

42 ¶ Nevertheless among the chief rulers also many believed on him; but because of the Pharisees they did not confess *him*, lest they should be put out of the synagogue:

43 For they loved the praise of men more than the praise of God.

44 ¶ Jesus cried and said, He that believeth on me, believeth not on me, but on him that sent me.

45 And he that seeth me seeth him that sent me.

46 I am come a light into the world, that whosoever believeth on me should not abide in darkness.

47 And if any man hear my words, and believe not, I judge him not: for I came not to judge the world, but to save the world.

48 He that rejecteth me, and receiveth not my words, hath one that judgeth him: the word that I have spoken, the same shall judge him in the last day.

49 For I have not spoken of myself; but the Father which sent me, he gave me a commandment, what I should say, and what I should speak.

50 And I know that his commandment is life everlasting: whatsoever I speak therefore, even as the Father said unto me, so I speak.

CHAPTER 13

NOW before the feast of the passover, when Jesus knew that his hour was come that he should depart out of this world unto the Father, having loved his own which were in the world, he loved them unto the end.

2 And supper being ended, the devil having now put into the heart of Judas Iscariot, Simon's *son*, to betray him;

3 Jesus knowing that the Father had given all things into his hands, and that he was come from God, and went to God;

4 He riseth from supper, and laid aside his garments; and took a towel, and girded himself.

5 After that he poureth water into a bason, and began to wash the disciples' feet, and to wipe *them* with the towel wherewith he was girded.

6 Then cometh he to Simon Peter: and Peter saith unto him, Lord, dost thou wash my feet?

7 Jesus answered and said unto him, What I do thou knowest not now; but thou shalt know hereafter.

8 Peter saith unto him, Thou shalt never wash my feet. Jesus answered him, If I wash thee not, thou hast no part with me.

9 Simon Peter saith unto him, Lord, not my feet only, but also *my* hands and *my* head.

10 Jesus saith to him, He that is

washed needeth not save to wash *his* feet, but is clean every whit: and ye are clean, but not all.

11 For he knew who should betray him; therefore said he, Ye are not all clean.

12 So after he had washed their feet, and had taken his garments, and was set down again, he said unto them, Know ye what I have done to you?

13 Ye call me Master and Lord: and ye say well; for *so* I am.

14 If I then, *your* Lord and Master, have washed your feet; ye also ought to wash one another's feet.

15 For I have given you an example, that ye should do as I have done to you.

16 Verily, verily, I say unto you, The servant is not greater than his lord; neither he that is sent greater than he that sent him.

17 If ye know these things, happy are ye if ye do them.

18 ¶ I speak not of you all: I know whom I have chosen: but that the scripture may be fulfilled, He that eateth bread with me hath lifted up his heel against me.

19 Now I tell you before it come, that, when it is come to pass, ye may believe that I am *he.*

20 Verily, verily, I say unto you, He that receiveth whomsoever I send receiveth me; and he that receiveth me receiveth him that sent me.

21 When Jesus had thus said, he was troubled in spirit, and testified, and said, Verily, verily, I say unto you, that one of you shall betray me.

22 Then the disciples looked one on another, doubting of whom he spake.

23 Now there was leaning on Jesus' bosom one of his disciples, whom Jesus loved.

24 Simon Peter therefore beckoned to him, that he should ask who it should be of whom he spake.

25 He then lying on Jesus' breast saith unto him, Lord, who is it?

26 Jesus answered, He it is, to whom I shall give a sop, when I have dipped *it.* And when he had dipped the sop, he gave *it* to Judas Iscariot, *the son* of Simon.

27 And after the sop Satan entered into him. Then said Jesus unto him, That thou doest, do quickly.

28 Now no man at the table knew for what intent he spake this unto him.

29 For some *of them* thought, because Judas had the bag, that Jesus had said unto him, Buy *those things* that we have need of against the feast; or, that he should give something to the poor.

30 He then having received the sop went immediately out: and it was night.

31 ¶ Therefore, when he was gone out, Jesus said, Now is the Son of man glorified, and God is glorified in him.

32 If God be glorified in him, God shall also glorify him in himself, and shall straightway glorify him.

33 Little children, yet a little while I am with you. Ye shall seek me: and as I said unto the Jews,

Whither I go, ye cannot come; so now I say to you.

34 A new commandment I give unto you, That ye love one another; as I have loved you, that ye also love one another.

35 By this shall all *men* know that ye are my disciples, if ye have love one to another.

36 ¶ Simon Peter said unto him, Lord, whither goest thou? Jesus answered him, Whither I go, thou canst not follow me now; but thou shalt follow me afterwards.

37 Peter said unto him, Lord, why cannot I follow thee now? I will lay down my life for thy sake.

38 Jesus answered him, Wilt thou lay down thy life for my sake? Verily, verily, I say unto thee, The cock shall not crow, till thou hast denied me thrice.

CHAPTER 14

LET not your heart be troubled: ye believe in God, believe also in me.

2 In my Father's house are many mansions: if *it were* not *so*, I would have told you. I go to prepare a place for you.

3 And if I go and prepare a place for you, I will come again, and receive you unto myself; that where I am, *there* ye may be also.

4 And whither I go ye know, and the way ye know.

5 Thomas saith unto him, Lord, we know not whither thou goest; and how can we know the way?

6 Jesus saith unto him, I am the way, the truth, and the life: no man cometh unto the Father, but by me.

7 If ye had known me, ye should have known my Father also: and from henceforth ye know him, and have seen him.

8 Philip saith unto him, Lord, shew us the Father, and it sufficeth us.

9 Jesus saith unto him, Have I been so long time with you, and yet hast thou not known me, Philip? he that hath seen me hath seen the Father; and how sayest thou *then*, Shew us the Father?

10 Believest thou not that I am in the Father, and the Father in me? the words that I speak unto you I speak not of myself: but the Father that dwelleth in me, he doeth the works.

11 Believe me that I *am* in the Father, and the Father in me: or else believe me for the very works' sake.

12 Verily, verily, I say unto you, He that believeth on me, the works that I do shall he do also; and greater *works* than these shall he do; because I go unto my Father.

13 And whatsoever ye shall ask in my name, that will I do, that the Father may be glorified in the Son.

14 If ye shall ask any thing in my name, I will do *it*.

15 ¶ If ye love me, keep my commandments.

16 And I will pray the Father, and he shall give you another Comforter, that he may abide with you for ever;

17 *Even* the Spirit of truth; whom the world cannot receive, because it seeth him not, neither knoweth him: but ye know him; for he dwelleth with you, and shall be in you.

18 I will not leave you comfortless: I will come to you.

19 Yet a little while, and the world seeth me no more; but ye see me: because I live, ye shall live also.

20 At that day ye shall know that I *am* in my Father, and ye in me, and I in you.

21 He that hath my commandments, and keepeth them, he it is that loveth me: and he that loveth me shall be loved of my Father, and I will love him, and will manifest myself to him.

22 Judas saith unto him, not Iscariot, Lord, how is it that thou wilt manifest thyself unto us, and not unto the world?

23 Jesus answered and said unto him, If a man love me, he will keep my words: and my Father will love him, and we will come unto him, and make our abode with him.

24 He that loveth me not keepeth not my sayings: and the word which ye hear is not mine, but the Father's which sent me.

25 These things have I spoken unto you, being *yet* present with you.

26 But the Comforter, *which is* the Holy Ghost, whom the Father will send in my name, he shall teach you all things, and bring all things to your remembrance, whatsoever I have said unto you.

27 Peace I leave with you, my peace I give unto you: not as the world giveth, give I unto you. Let not your heart be troubled, neither let it be afraid.

28 Ye have heard how I said unto you, I go away, and come *again* unto you. If ye loved me, ye would rejoice, because I said, I go unto the Father: for my Father is greater than I.

29 And now I have told you before it come to pass, that, when it is come to pass, ye might believe.

30 Hereafter I will not talk much with you: for the prince of this world cometh, and hath nothing in me.

31 But that the world may know that I love the Father; and as the Father gave me commandment, even so I do. Arise, let us go hence.

CHAPTER 15

I AM the true vine, and my Father is the husbandman.

2 Every branch in me that beareth not fruit he taketh away: and every *branch* that beareth fruit, he purgeth it, that it may bring forth more fruit.

3 Now ye are clean through the word which I have spoken unto you.

4 Abide in me, and I in you. As the branch cannot bear fruit of itself, except it abide in the vine; no more can ye, except ye abide in me.

5 I am the vine, ye *are* the branches: He that abideth in me, and I in him, the same bringeth forth much fruit: for without me ye can do nothing.

6 If a man abide not in me, he is cast forth as a branch, and is withered; and men gather them, and cast *them* into the fire, and they are burned.

7 If ye abide in me, and my

words abide in you, ye shall ask what ye will, and it shall be done unto you.

8 Herein is my Father glorified, that ye bear much fruit; so shall ye be my disciples.

9 As the Father hath loved me, so have I loved you: continue ye in my love.

10 If ye keep my commandments, ye shall abide in my love; even as I have kept my Father's commandments, and abide in his love.

11 These things have I spoken unto you, that my joy might remain in you, and *that* your joy might be full.

12 This is my commandment, That ye love one another, as I have loved you.

13 Greater love hath no man than this, that a man lay down his life for his friends.

14 Ye are my friends, if ye do whatsoever I command you.

15 Henceforth I call you not servants; for the servant knoweth not what his lord doeth: but I have called you friends; for all things that I have heard of my Father I have made known unto you.

16 Ye have not chosen me, but I have chosen you, and ordained you, that ye should go and bring forth fruit, and *that* your fruit should remain: that whatsoever ye shall ask of the Father in my name, he may give it you.

17 These things I command you, that ye love one another.

18 If the world hate you, ye know that it hated me before *it hated* you.

19 If ye were of the world, the world would love his own: but because ye are not of the world, but I have chosen you out of the world, therefore the world hateth you.

20 Remember the word that I said unto you, The servant is not greater than his lord. If they have persecuted me, they will also persecute you; if they have kept my saying, they will keep yours also.

21 But all these things will they do unto you for my name's sake, because they know not him that sent me.

22 If I had not come and spoken unto them, they had not had sin: but now they have no cloke for their sin.

23 He that hateth me hateth my Father also.

24 If I had not done among them the works which none other man did, they had not had sin: but now have they both seen and hated both me and my Father.

25 But *this cometh to pass*, that the word might be fulfilled that is written in their law, They hated me without a cause.

26 But when the Comforter is come, whom I will send unto you from the Father, *even* the Spirit of truth, which proceedeth from the Father, he shall testify of me:

27 And ye also shall bear witness, because ye have been with me from the beginning.

CHAPTER 16

THESE things have I spoken unto you, that ye should not be offended.

2 They shall put you out of the synagogues: yea, the time cometh, that whosoever killeth you will think that he doeth God service.

3 And these things will they do unto you, because they have not known the Father, nor me.

4 But these things have I told you, that when the time shall come, ye may remember that I told you of them. And these things I said not unto you at the beginning, because I was with you.

5 But now I go my way to him that sent me; and none of you asketh me, Whither goest thou?

6 But because I have said these things unto you, sorrow hath filled your heart.

7 Nevertheless I tell you the truth; It is expedient for you that I go away: for if I go not away, the Comforter will not come unto you; but if I depart, I will send him unto you.

8 And when he is come, he will reprove the world of sin, and of righteousness, and of judgment:

9 Of sin, because they believe not on me;

10 Of righteousness, because I go to my Father, and ye see me no more;

11 Of judgment, because the prince of this world is judged.

12 I have yet many things to say unto you, but ye cannot bear them now.

13 Howbeit when he, the Spirit of truth, is come, he will guide you into all truth: for he shall not speak of himself; but whatsoever he shall hear, *that* shall he speak: and he will shew you things to come.

14 He shall glorify me: for he shall receive of mine, and shall shew *it* unto you.

15 All things that the Father hath are mine: therefore said I, that he shall take of mine, and shall shew *it* unto you.

16 A little while, and ye shall not see me: and again, a little while, and ye shall see me, because I go to the Father.

17 Then said *some* of his disciples among themselves, What is this that he saith unto us, A little while, and ye shall not see me: and again, a little while, and ye shall see me: and, Because I go to the Father?

18 They said therefore, What is this that he saith, A little while? we cannot tell what he saith.

19 Now Jesus knew that they were desirous to ask him, and said unto them, Do ye enquire among yourselves of that I said, A little while, and ye shall not see me: and again, a little while, and ye shall see me?

20 Verily, verily, I say unto you, That ye shall weep and lament, but the world shall rejoice: and ye shall be sorrowful, but your sorrow shall be turned into joy.

21 A woman when she is in travail hath sorrow, because her hour is come: but as soon as she is delivered of the child, she remembereth no more the anguish, for joy that a man is born into the world.

22 And ye now therefore have sorrow: but I will see you again, and your heart shall rejoice, and

your joy no man taketh from you.

23 And in that day ye shall ask me nothing. Verily, verily, I say unto you, Whatsoever ye shall ask the Father in my name, he will give *it* you.

24 Hitherto have ye asked nothing in my name: ask, and ye shall receive, that your joy may be full.

25 These things have I spoken unto you in proverbs: but the time cometh, when I shall no more speak unto you in proverbs, but I shall shew you plainly of the Father.

26 At that day ye shall ask in my name: and I say not unto you, that I will pray the Father for you:

27 For the Father himself loveth you, because ye have loved me, and have believed that I came out from God.

28 I came forth from the Father, and am come into the world: again, I leave the world, and go to the Father.

29 His disciples said unto him, Lo, now speakest thou plainly, and speakest no proverb.

30 Now are we sure that thou knowest all things, and needest not that any man should ask thee: by this we believe that thou camest forth from God.

31 Jesus answered them, Do ye now believe?

32 Behold, the hour cometh, yea, is now come, that ye shall be scattered, every man to his own, and shall leave me alone: and yet I am not alone, because the Father is with me.

33 These things I have spoken unto you, that in me ye might have peace. In the world ye shall have tribulation: but be of good cheer; I have overcome the world.

CHAPTER 17

THESE words spake Jesus, and lifted up his eyes to heaven, and said, Father, the hour is come; glorify thy Son, that thy Son also may glorify thee:

2 As thou hast given him power over all flesh, that he should give eternal life to as many as thou hast given him.

3 And this is life eternal, that they might know thee the only true God, and Jesus Christ, whom thou hast sent.

4 I have glorified thee on the earth: I have finished the work which thou gavest me to do.

5 And now, O Father, glorify thou me with thine own self with the glory which I had with thee before the world was.

6 I have manifested thy name unto the men which thou gavest me out of the world: thine they were, and thou gavest them me; and they have kept thy word.

7 Now they have known that all things whatsoever thou hast given me are of thee.

8 For I have given unto them the words which thou gavest me; and they have received *them*, and have known surely that I came out from thee, and they have believed that thou didst send me.

9 I pray for them: I pray not for the world, but for them which thou hast given me; for they are thine.

10 And all mine are thine, and thine are mine; and I am glorified in them.

11 And now I am no more in the world, but these are in the world, and I come to thee. Holy Father, keep through thine own name those whom thou hast given me, that they may be one, as we *are*.

12 While I was with them in the world, I kept them in thy name: those that thou gavest me I have kept, and none of them is lost, but the son of perdition; that the scripture might be fulfilled.

13 And now come I to thee; and these things I speak in the world, that they might have my joy fulfilled in themselves.

14 I have given them thy word; and the world hath hated them, because they are not of the world, even as I am not of the world.

15 I pray not that thou shouldest take them out of the world, but that thou shouldest keep them from the evil.

16 They are not of the world, even as I am not of the world.

17 Sanctify them through thy truth: thy word is truth.

18 As thou hast sent me into the world, even so have I also sent them into the world.

19 And for their sakes I sanctify myself, that they also might be sanctified through the truth.

20 Neither pray I for these alone, but for them also which shall believe on me through their word;

21 That they all may be one; as thou, Father, *art* in me, and I in thee, that they also may be one in us: that the world may believe that thou hast sent me.

22 And the glory which thou gavest me I have given them; that they may be one, even as we are one:

23 I in them, and thou in me, that they may be made perfect in one; and that the world may know that thou hast sent me, and hast loved them, as thou hast loved me.

24 Father, I will that they also, whom thou hast given me, be with me where I am; that they may behold my glory, which thou hast given me: for thou lovedst me before the foundation of the world.

25 O righteous Father, the world hath not known thee: but I have known thee, and these have known that thou hast sent me.

26 And I have declared unto them thy name, and will declare *it*: that the love wherewith thou hast loved me may be in them, and I in them.

CHAPTER 18

WHEN Jesus had spoken these words, he went forth with his disciples over the brook Cedron, where was a garden, into the which he entered, and his disciples.

2 And Judas also, which betrayed him, knew the place: for Jesus ofttimes resorted thither with his disciples.

3 Judas then, having received a band *of men* and officers from the chief priests and Pharisees, cometh thither with lanterns and torches and weapons.

4 Jesus therefore, knowing all things that should come upon him, went forth, and said unto them, Whom seek ye?

5 They answered him, Jesus of Nazareth. Jesus saith unto them, I am *he*. And Judas also, which betrayed him, stood with them.

6 As soon then as he had said unto them, I am *he*, they went backward, and fell to the ground.

7 Then asked he them again, Whom seek ye? And they said, Jesus of Nazareth.

8 Jesus answered, I have told you that I am *he*: if therefore ye seek me, let these go their way:

9 That the saying might be fulfilled, which he spake, Of them which thou gavest me have I lost none.

10 Then Simon Peter having a sword drew it, and smote the high priest's servant, and cut off his right ear. The servant's name was Malchus.

11 Then said Jesus unto Peter, Put up thy sword into the sheath: the cup which my Father hath given me, shall I not drink it?

12 Then the band and the captain and officers of the Jews took Jesus, and bound him,

13 And led him away to Annas first; for he was father in law to Caiaphas, which was the high priest that same year.

14 Now Caiaphas was he, which gave counsel to the Jews, that it was expedient that one man should die for the people.

15 ¶ And Simon Peter followed Jesus, and *so did* another disciple: that disciple was known unto the high priest, and went in with Jesus into the palace of the high priest.

16 But Peter stood at the door without. Then went out that other disciple, which was known unto the high priest, and spake unto her that kept the door, and brought in Peter.

17 Then saith the damsel that kept the door unto Peter, Art not thou also *one* of this man's disciples? He saith, I am not.

18 And the servants and officers stood there, who had made a fire of coals; for it was cold: and they warmed themselves: and Peter stood with them, and warmed himself.

19 ¶ The high priest then asked Jesus of his disciples, and of his doctrine.

20 Jesus answered him, I spake openly to the world; I ever taught in the synagogue, and in the temple, whither the Jews always resort; and in secret have I said nothing.

21 Why askest thou me? ask them which heard me, what I have said unto them: behold, they know what I said.

22 And when he had thus spoken, one of the officers which stood by struck Jesus with the palm of his hand, saying, Answerest thou the high priest so?

23 Jesus answered him, If I have spoken evil, bear witness of the evil: but if well, why smitest thou me?

24 Now Annas had sent him bound unto Caiaphas the high priest.

25 And Simon Peter stood and warmed himself. They said

therefore unto him, Art not thou also *one* of his disciples? He denied *it*, and said, I am not.

26 One of the servants of the high priest, being *his* kinsman whose ear Peter cut off, saith, Did not I see thee in the garden with him?

27 Peter then denied again: and immediately the cock crew.

28 ¶ Then led they Jesus from Caiaphas unto the hall of judgment: and it was early; and they themselves went not into the judgment hall, lest they should be defiled; but that they might eat the passover.

29 Pilate then went out unto them, and said, What accusation bring ye against this man?

30 They answered and said unto him, If he were not a malefactor, we would not have delivered him up unto thee.

31 Then said Pilate unto them, Take ye him, and judge him according to your law. The Jews therefore said unto him, It is not lawful for us to put any man to death:

32 That the saying of Jesus might be fulfilled, which he spake, signifying what death he should die.

33 Then Pilate entered into the judgment hall again, and called Jesus, and said unto him, Art thou the King of the Jews?

34 Jesus answered him, Sayest thou this thing of thyself, or did others tell it thee of me?

35 Pilate answered, Am I a Jew? Thine own nation and the chief priests have delivered thee unto me: what hast thou done?

36 Jesus answered, My kingdom is not of this world: if my kingdom were of this world, then would my servants fight, that I should not be delivered to the Jews: but now is my kingdom not from hence.

37 Pilate therefore said unto him, Art thou a king then? Jesus answered, Thou sayest that I am a king. To this end was I born, and for this cause came I into the world, that I should bear witness unto the truth. Every one that is of the truth heareth my voice.

38 Pilate saith unto him, What is truth? And when he had said this, he went out again unto the Jews, and saith unto them, I find in him no fault *at all*.

39 But ye have a custom, that I should release unto you one at the passover: will ye therefore that I release unto you the King of the Jews?

40 Then cried they all again, saying, Not this man, but Barabbas. Now Barabbas was a robber.

CHAPTER 19

THEN Pilate therefore took Jesus, and scourged *him*.

2 And the soldiers platted a crown of thorns, and put *it* on his head, and they put on him a purple robe,

3 And said, Hail, King of the Jews! and they smote him with their hands.

4 Pilate therefore went forth again, and saith unto them, Behold, I bring him forth to you, that ye may know that I find no fault in him.

5 Then came Jesus forth, wear-

ing the crown of thorns, and the purple robe. And *Pilate* saith unto them, Behold the man!

6 When the chief priests therefore and officers saw him, they cried out, saying, Crucify *him*, crucify *him*. Pilate saith unto them, Take ye him, and crucify *him*: for I find no fault in him.

7 The Jews answered him, We have a law, and by our law he ought to die, because he made himself the Son of God.

8 ¶ When Pilate therefore heard that saying, he was the more afraid;

9 And went again into the judgment hall, and saith unto Jesus, Whence art thou? But Jesus gave him no answer.

10 Then saith Pilate unto him, Speakest thou not unto me? knowest thou not that I have power to crucify thee, and have power to release thee?

11 Jesus answered, Thou couldest have no power *at all* against me, except it were given thee from above: therefore he that delivered me unto thee hath the greater sin.

12 And from thenceforth Pilate sought to release him: but the Jews cried out, saying, If thou let this man go, thou art not Caesar's friend: whosoever maketh himself a king speaketh against Caesar.

13 ¶ When Pilate therefore heard that saying, he brought Jesus forth, and sat down in the judgment seat in a place that is called the Pavement, but in the Hebrew, Gabbatha.

14 And it was the preparation of the passover, and about the sixth hour: and he saith unto the Jews, Behold your King!

15 But they cried out, Away with *him*, away with *him*, crucify him. Pilate saith unto them, Shall I crucify your King? The chief priests answered, We have no king but Caesar.

16 Then delivered he him therefore unto them to be crucified. And they took Jesus, and led *him* away.

17 And he bearing his cross went forth into a place called *the place* of a skull, which is called in the Hebrew Golgotha:

18 Where they crucified him, and two other with him, on either side one, and Jesus in the midst.

19 ¶ And Pilate wrote a title, and put *it* on the cross. And the writing was, JESUS OF NAZARETH THE KING OF THE JEWS.

20 This title then read many of the Jews: for the place where Jesus was crucified was nigh to the city: and it was written in Hebrew, *and* Greek, *and* Latin.

21 Then said the chief priests of the Jews to Pilate, Write not, The King of the Jews; but that he said, I am King of the Jews.

22 Pilate answered, What I have written I have written.

23 ¶ Then the soldiers, when they had crucified Jesus, took his garments, and made four parts, to every soldier a part; and also *his* coat: now the coat was without seam, woven from the top throughout.

24 They said therefore among themselves, Let us not rend it, but cast lots for it, whose it shall be: that the scripture might be

fulfilled, which saith, They parted my raiment among them, and for my vesture they did cast lots. These things therefore the soldiers did.

25 ¶ Now there stood by the cross of Jesus his mother, and his mother's sister, Mary the *wife* of Cleophas, and Mary Magdalene.

26 When Jesus therefore saw his mother, and the disciple standing by, whom he loved, he saith unto his mother, Woman, behold thy son!

27 Then saith he to the disciple, Behold thy mother! And from that hour that disciple took her unto his own *home*.

28 ¶ After this, Jesus knowing that all things were now accomplished, that the scripture might be fulfilled, saith, I thirst.

29 Now there was set a vessel full of vinegar: and they filled a spunge with vinegar, and put *it* upon hyssop, and put *it* to his mouth.

30 When Jesus therefore had received the vinegar, he said, It is finished: and he bowed his head, and gave up the ghost.

31 The Jews therefore, because it was the preparation, that the bodies should not remain upon the cross on the sabbath day, (for that sabbath day was an high day,) besought Pilate that their legs might be broken, and *that* they might be taken away.

32 Then came the soldiers, and brake the legs of the first, and of the other which was crucified with him.

33 But when they came to Jesus, and saw that he was dead already, they brake not his legs:

34 But one of the soldiers with a spear pierced his side, and forthwith came there out blood and water.

35 And he that saw *it* bare record, and his record is true: and he knoweth that he saith true, that ye might believe.

36 For these things were done, that the scripture should be fulfilled, A bone of him shall not be broken.

37 And again another scripture saith, They shall look on him whom they pierced.

38 ¶ And after this Joseph of Arimathaea, being a disciple of Jesus, but secretly for fear of the Jews, besought Pilate that he might take away the body of Jesus: and Pilate gave *him* leave. He came therefore, and took the body of Jesus.

39 And there came also Nicodemus, which at the first came to Jesus by night, and brought a mixture of myrrh and aloes, about an hundred pound *weight*.

40 Then took they the body of Jesus, and wound it in linen clothes with the spices, as the manner of the Jews is to bury.

41 Now in the place where he was crucified there was a garden; and in the garden a new sepulchre, wherein was never man yet laid.

42 There laid they Jesus therefore because of the Jews' preparation *day*; for the sepulchre was nigh at hand.

CHAPTER 20

THE first *day* of the week cometh Mary Magdalene early, when it was yet dark, unto the sepulchre, and seeth the stone taken away from the sepulchre.

2 Then she runneth, and cometh to Simon Peter, and to the other disciple, whom Jesus loved, and saith unto them, They have taken away the Lord out of the sepulchre, and we know not where they have laid him.

3 Peter therefore went forth, and that other disciple, and came to the sepulchre.

4 So they ran both together: and the other disciple did outrun Peter, and came first to the sepulchre.

5 And he stooping down, *and looking in*, saw the linen clothes lying; yet went he not in.

6 Then cometh Simon Peter following him, and went into the sepulchre, and seeth the linen clothes lie,

7 And the napkin, that was about his head, not lying with the linen clothes, but wrapped together in a place by itself.

8 Then went in also that other disciple, which came first to the sepulchre, and he saw, and believed.

9 For as yet they knew not the scripture, that he must rise again from the dead.

10 Then the disciples went away again unto their own home.

11 ¶ But Mary stood without at the sepulchre weeping: and as she wept, she stooped down, *and looked* into the sepulchre,

12 And seeth two angels in white sitting, the one at the head, and the other at the feet, where the body of Jesus had lain.

13 And they say unto her, Woman, why weepest thou? She saith unto them, Because they have taken away my Lord, and I know not where they have laid him.

14 And when she had thus said, she turned herself back, and saw Jesus standing, and knew not that it was Jesus.

15 Jesus saith unto her, Woman, why weepest thou? whom seekest thou? She, supposing him to be the gardener, saith unto him, Sir, if thou have borne him hence, tell me where thou hast laid him, and I will take him away.

16 Jesus saith unto her, Mary. She turned herself, and saith unto him, Rabboni; which is to say, Master.

17 Jesus saith unto her, Touch me not; for I am not yet ascended to my Father: but go to my brethren, and say unto them, I ascend unto my Father, and your Father; and *to* my God, and your God.

18 Mary Magdalene came and told the disciples that she had seen the Lord, and *that* he had spoken these things unto her.

19 ¶ Then the same day at evening, being the first *day* of the week, when the doors were shut where the disciples were assembled for fear of the Jews, came Jesus and stood in the midst, and saith unto them, Peace *be* unto you.

20 And when he had so said, he shewed unto them *his* hands and his side. Then were the disciples glad, when they saw the Lord.

21 Then said Jesus to them again, Peace *be* unto you: as *my*

Father hath sent me, even so send I you.

22 And when he had said this, he breathed on *them*, and saith unto them, Receive ye the Holy Ghost:

23 Whose soever sins ye remit, they are remitted unto them; *and* whose soever *sins* ye retain, they are retained.

24 ¶ But Thomas, one of the twelve, called Didymus, was not with them when Jesus came.

25 The other disciples therefore said unto him, We have seen the Lord. But he said unto them, Except I shall see in his hands the print of the nails, and put my finger into the print of the nails, and thrust my hand into his side, I will not believe.

26 ¶ And after eight days again his disciples were within, and Thomas with them: *then* came Jesus, the doors being shut, and stood in the midst, and said, Peace *be* unto you.

27 Then saith he to Thomas, Reach hither thy finger, and behold my hands; and reach hither thy hand, and thrust *it* into my side: and be not faithless, but believing.

28 And Thomas answered and said unto him, My Lord and my God.

29 Jesus saith unto him, Thomas, because thou hast seen me, thou hast believed: blessed *are* they that have not seen, and *yet* have believed.

30 ¶ And many other signs truly did Jesus in the presence of his disciples, which are not written in this book:

31 But these are written, that ye might believe that Jesus is the Christ, the Son of God; and that believing ye might have life through his name.

CHAPTER 21

AFTER these things Jesus shewed himself again to the disciples at the sea of Tiberias; and on this wise shewed he *himself*.

2 There were together Simon Peter, and Thomas called Didymus, and Nathanael of Cana in Galilee, and the *sons* of Zebedee, and two other of his disciples.

3 Simon Peter saith unto them, I go a fishing. They say unto him, We also go with thee. They went forth, and entered into a ship immediately; and that night they caught nothing.

4 But when the morning was now come, Jesus stood on the shore: but the disciples knew not that it was Jesus.

5 Then Jesus saith unto them, Children, have ye any meat? They answered him, No.

6 And he said unto them, Cast the net on the right side of the ship, and ye shall find. They cast therefore, and now they were not able to draw it for the multitude of fishes.

7 Therefore that disciple whom Jesus loved saith unto Peter, It is the Lord. Now when Simon Peter heard that it was the Lord, he girt *his* fisher's coat *unto him*, (for he was naked,) and did cast himself into the sea.

8 And the other disciples came in a little ship; (for they were not

far from land, but as it were two hundred cubits,) dragging the net with fishes.

9 As soon then as they were come to land, they saw a fire of coals there, and fish laid thereon, and bread.

10 Jesus saith unto them, Bring of the fish which ye have now caught.

11 Simon Peter went up, and drew the net to land full of great fishes, an hundred and fifty and three: and for all there were so many, yet was not the net broken.

12 Jesus saith unto them, Come *and* dine. And none of the disciples durst ask him, Who art thou? knowing that it was the Lord.

13 Jesus then cometh, and taketh bread, and giveth them, and fish likewise.

14 This is now the third time that Jesus shewed himself to his disciples, after that he was risen from the dead.

15 ¶ So when they had dined, Jesus saith to Simon Peter, Simon, *son* of Jonas, lovest thou me more than these? He saith unto him, Yea, Lord; thou knowest that I love thee. He saith unto him, Feed my lambs.

16 He saith to him again the second time, Simon, *son* of Jonas, lovest thou me? He saith unto him, Yea, Lord; thou knowest that I love thee. He saith unto him, Feed my sheep.

17 He saith unto him the third time, Simon, *son* of Jonas, lovest thou me? Peter was grieved because he said unto him the third time, Lovest thou me? And he

said unto him, Lord, thou knowest all things; thou knowest that I love thee. Jesus saith unto him, Feed my sheep.

18 Verily, verily, I say unto thee, When thou wast young, thou girdedst thyself, and walkedst whither thou wouldest: but when thou shalt be old, thou shalt stretch forth thy hands, and another shall gird thee, and carry *thee* whither thou wouldest not.

19 This spake he, signifying by what death he should glorify God. And when he had spoken this, he saith unto him, Follow me.

20 Then Peter, turning about, seeth the disciple whom Jesus loved following; which also leaned on his breast at supper, and said, Lord, which is he that betrayeth thee?

21 Peter seeing him saith to Jesus, Lord, and what *shall* this man *do*?

22 Jesus saith unto him, If I will that he tarry till I come, what *is that* to thee? follow thou me.

23 Then went this saying abroad among the brethren, that that disciple should not die: yet Jesus said not unto him, He shall not die; but, If I will that he tarry till I come, what *is that* to thee?

24 This is the disciple which testifieth of these things, and wrote these things: and we know that his testimony is true.

25 And there are also many other things which Jesus did, the which, if they should be written every one, I suppose that even the world itself could not contain the books that should be written. Amen.

ROMANS

PAUL, a servant of Jesus Christ, called *to be* an apostle, separated unto the gospel of God,

2 (Which he had promised afore by his prophets in the holy scriptures,)

3 Concerning his Son Jesus Christ our Lord, which was made of the seed of David according to the flesh;

4 And declared *to be* the Son of God with power, according to the spirit of holiness, by the resurrection from the dead:

5 By whom we have received grace and apostleship, for obedience to the faith among all nations, for his name:

6 Among whom are ye also the called of Jesus Christ:

7 To all that be in Rome, beloved of God, called *to be* saints: Grace to you and peace from God our Father, and the Lord Jesus Christ.

8 First, I thank my God through Jesus Christ for you all, that your faith is spoken of throughout the whole world.

9 For God is my witness, whom I serve with my spirit in the gospel of his Son, that without ceasing I make mention of you always in my prayers;

10 Making request, if by any means now at length I might have a prosperous journey by the will of God to come unto you.

11 For I long to see you, that I may impart unto you some spiritual gift, to the end ye may be established;

12 That is, that I may be comforted together with you by the mutual faith both of you and me.

13 Now I would not have you ignorant, brethren, that oftentimes I purposed to come unto you, (but was let hitherto,) that I might have some fruit among you also, even as among other Gentiles.

14 I am debtor both to the Greeks, and to the Barbarians; both to the wise, and to the unwise.

15 So, as much as in me is, I am ready to preach the gospel to you that are at Rome also.

16 For I am not ashamed of the gospel of Christ: for it is the power of God unto salvation to every one that believeth; to the Jew first, and also to the Greek.

17 For therein is the righteousness of God revealed from faith to faith: as it is written, The just shall live by faith.

18 For the wrath of God is revealed from heaven against all ungodliness and unrighteousness of men, who hold the truth in unrighteousness;

19 Because that which may be known of God is manifest in them; for God hath shewed *it* unto them.

20 For the invisible things of him from the creation of the world are clearly seen, being

understood by the things that are made, *even* his eternal power and Godhead; so that they are without excuse:

21 Because that, when they knew God, they glorified *him* not as God, neither were thankful; but became vain in their imaginations, and their foolish heart was darkened.

22 Professing themselves to be wise, they became fools,

23 And changed the glory of the uncorruptible God into an image made like to corruptible man, and to birds, and fourfooted beasts, and creeping things.

24 Wherefore God also gave them up to uncleanness through the lusts of their own hearts, to dishonour their own bodies between themselves:

25 Who changed the truth of God into a lie, and worshipped and served the creature more than the Creator, who is blessed for ever. Amen.

26 For this cause God gave them up unto vile affections: for even their women did change the natural use into that which is against nature:

27 And likewise also the men, leaving the natural use of the woman, burned in their lust one toward another; men with men working that which is unseemly, and receiving in themselves that recompence of their error which was meet.

28 And even as they did not like to retain God in *their* knowledge, God gave them over to a reprobate mind, to do those things which are not convenient;

29 Being filled with all unrighteousness, fornication, wickedness, covetousness, maliciousness; full of envy, murder, debate, deceit, malignity; whisperers,

30 Backbiters, haters of God, despiteful, proud, boasters, inventors of evil things, disobedient to parents,

31 Without understanding, covenantbreakers, without natural affection, implacable, unmerciful:

32 Who knowing the judgment of God, that they which commit such things are worthy of death, not only do the same, but have pleasure in them that do them.

CHAPTER 2

THEREFORE thou art inexcusable, O man, whosoever thou art that judgest: for wherein thou judgest another, thou condemnest thyself; for thou that judgest doest the same things.

2 But we are sure that the judgment of God is according to truth against them which commit such things.

3 And thinkest thou this, O man, that judgest them which do such things, and doest the same, that thou shalt escape the judgment of God?

4 Or despisest thou the riches of his goodness and forbearance and longsuffering; not knowing that the goodness of God leadeth thee to repentance?

5 But after thy hardness and impenitent heart treasurest up unto thyself wrath against the day of wrath and revelation of the righteous judgment of God;

6 Who will render to every man according to his deeds:

7 To them who by patient continuance in well doing seek for glory and honour and immortality, eternal life:

8 But unto them that are contentious, and do not obey the truth, but obey unrighteousness, indignation and wrath,

9 Tribulation and anguish, upon every soul of man that doeth evil, of the Jew first, and also of the Gentile;

10 But glory, honour, and peace, to every man that worketh good, to the Jew first, and also to the Gentile:

11 For there is no respect of persons with God.

12 For as many as have sinned without law shall also perish without law: and as many as have sinned in the law shall be judged by the law;

13 (For not the hearers of the law *are* just before God, but the doers of the law shall be justified.

14 For when the Gentiles, which have not the law, do by nature the things contained in the law, these, having not the law, are a law unto themselves:

15 Which shew the work of the law written in their hearts, their conscience also bearing witness, and *their* thoughts the mean while accusing or else excusing one another;)

16 In the day when God shall judge the secrets of men by Jesus Christ according to my gospel.

17 Behold, thou art called a Jew, and restest in the law, and makest thy boast of God,

18 And knowest *his* will, and approvest the things that are more excellent, being instructed out of the law;

19 And art confident that thou thyself art a guide of the blind, a light of them which are in darkness,

20 An instructor of the foolish, a teacher of babes, which hast the form of knowledge and of the truth in the law.

21 Thou therefore which teachest another, teachest thou not thyself? thou that preachest a man should not steal, dost thou steal?

22 Thou that sayest a man should not commit adultery, dost thou commit adultery? thou that abhorrest idols, dost thou commit sacrilege?

23 Thou that makest thy boast of the law, through breaking the law dishonourest thou God?

24 For the name of God is blasphemed among the Gentiles through you, as it is written.

25 For circumcision verily profiteth, if thou keep the law: but if thou be a breaker of the law, thy circumcision is made uncircumcision.

26 Therefore if the uncircumcision keep the righteousness of the law, shall not his uncircumcision be counted for circumcision?

27 And shall not uncircumcision which is by nature, if it fulfil the law, judge thee, who by the letter and circumcision dost transgress the law?

28 For he is not a Jew, which is one outwardly; neither *is that* circumcision, which is outward in the flesh:

29 But he *is* a Jew, which is one inwardly; and circumcision *is that* of the heart, in the spirit, *and* not in the letter; whose praise *is* not of men, but of God.

CHAPTER 3

WHAT advantage then hath the Jew? or what profit *is there* of circumcision?

2 Much every way: chiefly, because that unto them were committed the oracles of God.

3 For what if some did not believe? shall their unbelief make the faith of God without effect?

4 God forbid: yea, let God be true, but every man a liar; as it is written, That thou mightest be justified in thy sayings, and mightest overcome when thou art judged.

5 But if our unrighteousness commend the righteousness of God, what shall we say? *Is* God unrighteous who taketh vengeance? (I speak as a man)

6 God forbid: for then how shall God judge the world?

7 For if the truth of God hath more abounded through my lie unto his glory; why yet am I also judged as a sinner?

8 And not *rather*, (as we be slanderously reported, and as some affirm that we say,) Let us do evil, that good may come? whose damnation is just.

9 What then? are we better *than they*? No, in no wise: for we have before proved both Jews and Gentiles, that they are all under sin;

10 As it is written, There is none righteous, no, not one:

11 There is none that understandeth, there is none that seeketh after God.

12 They are all gone out of the way, they are together become unprofitable; there is none that doeth good, no, not one.

13 Their throat *is* an open sepulchre; with their tongues they have used deceit; the poison of asps *is* under their lips:

14 Whose mouth *is* full of cursing and bitterness:

15 Their feet *are* swift to shed blood:

16 Destruction and misery *are* in their ways:

17 And the way of peace have they not known:

18 There is no fear of God before their eyes.

19 Now we know that what things soever the law saith, it saith to them who are under the law: that every mouth may be stopped, and all the world may become guilty before God.

20 Therefore by the deeds of the law there shall no flesh be justified in his sight: for by the law *is* the knowledge of sin.

21 But now the righteousness of God without the law is manifested, being witnessed by the law and the prophets;

22 Even the righteousness of God *which is* by faith of Jesus Christ unto all and upon all them that believe: for there is no difference:

23 For all have sinned, and come short of the glory of God;

24 Being justified freely by his grace through the redemption that is in Christ Jesus:

25 Whom God hath set forth *to*

be a propitiation through faith in his blood, to declare his righteousness for the remission of sins that are past, through the forbearance of God;

26 To declare, *I say*, at this time his righteousness: that he might be just, and the justifier of him which believeth in Jesus.

27 Where *is* boasting then? It is excluded. By what law? of works? Nay: but by the law of faith.

28 Therefore we conclude that a man is justified by faith without the deeds of the law.

29 *Is he* the God of the Jews only? *is he* not also of the Gentiles? Yes, of the Gentiles also:

30 Seeing *it is* one God, which shall justify the circumcision by faith, and uncircumcision through faith.

31 Do we then make void the law through faith? God forbid: yea, we establish the law.

CHAPTER 4

WHAT shall we say then that Abraham our father, as pertaining to the flesh, hath found?

2 For if Abraham were justified by works, he hath *whereof* to glory; but not before God.

3 For what saith the scripture? Abraham believed God, and it was counted unto him for righteousness.

4 Now to him that worketh is the reward not reckoned of grace, but of debt.

5 But to him that worketh not, but believeth on him that justifieth the ungodly, his faith is counted for righteousness.

6 Even as David also describeth the blessedness of the man, unto whom God imputeth righteousness without works,

7 *Saying*, Blessed *are* they whose iniquities are forgiven, and whose sins are covered.

8 Blessed *is* the man to whom the Lord will not impute sin.

9 *Cometh* this blessedness then upon the circumcision *only*, or upon the uncircumcision also? for we say that faith was reckoned to Abraham for righteousness.

10 How was it then reckoned? when he was in circumcision, or in uncircumcision? Not in circumcision, but in uncircumcision.

11 And he received the sign of circumcision, a seal of the righteousness of the faith which *he had yet* being uncircumcised: that he might be the father of all them that believe, though they be not circumcised; that righteousness might be imputed unto them also:

12 And the father of circumcision to them who are not of the circumcision only, but who also walk in the steps of that faith of our father Abraham, which *he had* being *yet* uncircumcised.

13 For the promise, that he should be the heir of the world, *was* not to Abraham, or to his seed, through the law, but through the righteousness of faith.

14 For if they which are of the law *be* heirs, faith is made void, and the promise made of none effect:

15 Because the law worketh wrath: for where no law is, *there is* no transgression.

16 Therefore *it is* of faith, that *it might be* by grace; to the end the promise might be sure to all the seed; not to that only which is of the law, but to that also which is of the faith of Abraham; who is the father of us all,

17 (As it is written, I have made thee a father of many nations,) before him whom he believed, *even* God, who quickeneth the dead, and calleth those things which be not as though they were.

18 Who against hope believed in hope, that he might become the father of many nations, according to that which was spoken, So shall thy seed be.

19 And being not weak in faith, he considered not his own body now dead, when he was about an hundred years old, neither yet the deadness of Sara's womb:

20 He staggered not at the promise of God through unbelief; but was strong in faith, giving glory to God;

21 And being fully persuaded that, what he had promised, he was able also to perform.

22 And therefore it was imputed to him for righteousness.

23 Now it was not written for his sake alone, that it was imputed to him;

24 But for us also, to whom it shall be imputed, if we believe on him that raised up Jesus our Lord from the dead;

25 Who was delivered for our offences, and was raised again for our justification.

CHAPTER 5

THEREFORE being justified by faith, we have peace with God through our Lord Jesus Christ;

2 By whom also we have access by faith into this grace wherein we stand, and rejoice in hope of the glory of God.

3 And not only *so*, but we glory in tribulations also: knowing that tribulation worketh patience;

4 And patience, experience; and experience, hope:

5 And hope maketh not ashamed; because the love of God is shed abroad in our hearts by the Holy Ghost which is given unto us.

6 For when we were yet without strength, in due time Christ died for the ungodly.

7 For scarcely for a righteous man will one die: yet peradventure for a good man some would even dare to die.

8 But God commendeth his love toward us, in that, while we were yet sinners, Christ died for us.

9 Much more then, being now justified by his blood, we shall be saved from wrath through him.

10 For if, when we were enemies, we were reconciled to God by the death of his Son, much more, being reconciled, we shall be saved by his life.

11 And not only *so*, but we also joy in God through our Lord Jesus Christ, by whom we have now received the atonement.

12 Wherefore, as by one man sin entered into the world, and death by sin; and so death passed

upon all men, for that all have sinned:

13 (For until the law sin was in the world: but sin is not imputed when there is no law.

14 Nevertheless death reigned from Adam to Moses, even over them that had not sinned after the similitude of Adam's transgression, who is the figure of him that was to come.

15 But not as the offence, so also *is* the free gift. For if through the offence of one many be dead, much more the grace of God, and the gift by grace, *which is* by one man, Jesus Christ, hath abounded unto many.

16 And not as *it was* by one that sinned, *so is* the gift: for the judgment *was* by one to condemnation, but the free gift *is* of many offences unto justification.

17 For if by one man's offence death reigned by one; much more they which receive abundance of grace and of the gift of righteousness shall reign in life by one, Jesus Christ.)

18 Therefore as by the offence of one *judgment came* upon all men to condemnation; even so by the righteousness of one *the free gift came* upon all men unto justification of life.

19 For as by one man's disobedience many were made sinners, so by the obedience of one shall many be made righteous.

20 Moreover the law entered, that the offence might abound. But where sin abounded, grace did much more abound:

21 That as sin hath reigned unto death, even so might grace reign through righteousness unto eternal life by Jesus Christ our Lord.

CHAPTER 6

WHAT shall we say then? Shall we continue in sin, that grace may abound?

2 God forbid. How shall we, that are dead to sin, live any longer therein?

3 Know ye not, that so many of us as were baptized into Jesus Christ were baptized into his death?

4 Therefore we are buried with him by baptism into death: that like as Christ was raised up from the dead by the glory of the Father, even so we also should walk in newness of life.

5 For if we have been planted together in the likeness of his death, we shall be also *in the likeness* of *his* resurrection:

6 Knowing this, that our old man is crucified with *him*, that the body of sin might be destroyed, that henceforth we should not serve sin.

7 For he that is dead is freed from sin.

8 Now if we be dead with Christ, we believe that we shall also live with him:

9 Knowing that Christ being raised from the dead dieth no more; death hath no more dominion over him.

10 For in that he died, he died unto sin once: but in that he liveth, he liveth unto God.

11 Likewise reckon ye also yourselves to be dead indeed unto sin, but alive unto God through Jesus Christ our Lord.

12 Let not sin therefore reign in your mortal body, that ye should obey it in the lusts thereof.

13 Neither yield ye your members *as* instruments of unrighteousness unto sin: but yield yourselves unto God, as those that are alive from the dead, and your members *as* instruments of righteousness unto God.

14 For sin shall not have dominion over you: for ye are not under the law, but under grace.

15 What then? shall we sin, because we are not under the law, but under grace? God forbid.

16 Know ye not, that to whom ye yield yourselves servants to obey, his servants ye are to whom ye obey; whether of sin unto death, or of obedience unto righteousness?

17 But God be thanked, that ye were the servants of sin, but ye have obeyed from the heart that form of doctrine which was delivered you.

18 Being then made free from sin, ye became the servants of righteousness.

19 I speak after the manner of men because of the infirmity of your flesh: for as ye have yielded your members servants to uncleanness and to iniquity unto iniquity; even so now yield your members servants to righteousness unto holiness.

20 For when ye were the servants of sin, ye were free from righteousness.

21 What fruit had ye then in those things whereof ye are now ashamed? for the end of those things *is* death.

22 But now being made free from sin, and become servants to God, ye have your fruit unto holiness, and the end everlasting life.

23 For the wages of sin *is* death; but the gift of God *is* eternal life through Jesus Christ our Lord.

CHAPTER 7

KNOW ye not, brethren, (for I speak to them that know the law,) how that the law hath dominion over a man as long as he liveth?

2 For the woman which hath an husband is bound by the law to *her* husband so long as he liveth; but if the husband be dead, she is loosed from the law of *her* husband.

3 So then if, while *her* husband liveth, she be married to another man, she shall be called an adulteress: but if her husband be dead, she is free from that law; so that she is no adulteress, though she be married to another man.

4 Wherefore, my brethren, ye also are become dead to the law by the body of Christ; that ye should be married to another, *even* to him who is raised from the dead, that we should bring forth fruit unto God.

5 For when we were in the flesh, the motions of sins, which were by the law, did work in our members to bring forth fruit unto death.

6 But now we are delivered from the law, that being dead wherein we were held; that we should serve in newness of spirit, and not *in* the oldness of the letter.

7 What shall we say then? *Is* the

law sin? God forbid. Nay, I had not known sin, but by the law: for I had not known lust, except the law had said, Thou shalt not covet.

8 But sin, taking occasion by the commandment, wrought in me all manner of concupiscence. For without the law sin *was* dead.

9 For I was alive without the law once: but when the commandment came, sin revived, and I died.

10 And the commandment, which *was ordained* to life, I found *to be* unto death.

11 For sin, taking occasion by the commandment, deceived me, and by it slew *me*.

12 Wherefore the law *is* holy, and the commandment holy, and just, and good.

13 Was then that which is good made death unto me? God forbid. But sin, that it might appear sin, working death in me by that which is good; that sin by the commandment might become exceeding sinful.

14 For we know that the law is spiritual: but I am carnal, sold under sin.

15 For that which I do I allow not: for what I would, that do I not; but what I hate, that do I.

16 If then I do that which I would not, I consent unto the law that *it is* good.

17 Now then it is no more I that do it, but sin that dwelleth in me.

18 For I know that in me (that is, in my flesh,) dwelleth no good thing: for to will is present with me; but *how* to perform that which is good I find not.

19 For the good that I would I do not: but the evil which I would not, that I do.

20 Now if I do that I would not, it is no more I that do it, but sin that dwelleth in me.

21 I find then a law, that, when I would do good, evil is present with me.

22 For I delight in the law of God after the inward man:

23 But I see another law in my members, warring against the law of my mind, and bringing me into captivity to the law of sin which is in my members.

24 O wretched man that I am! who shall deliver me from the body of this death?

25 I thank God through Jesus Christ our Lord. So then with the mind I myself serve the law of God; but with the flesh the law of sin.

CHAPTER 8

*T*HERE is therefore now no condemnation to them which are in Christ Jesus, who walk not after the flesh, but after the Spirit.

2 For the law of the Spirit of life in Christ Jesus hath made me free from the law of sin and death.

3 For what the law could not do, in that it was weak through the flesh, God sending his own Son in the likeness of sinful flesh, and for sin, condemned sin in the flesh:

4 That the righteousness of the law might be fulfilled in us, who walk not after the flesh, but after the Spirit.

5 For they that are after the flesh

do mind the things of the flesh; but they that are after the Spirit the things of the Spirit.

6 For to be carnally minded *is* death; but to be spiritually minded *is* life and peace.

7 Because the carnal mind *is* enmity against God: for it is not subject to the law of God, neither indeed can be.

8 So then they that are in the flesh cannot please God.

9 But ye are not in the flesh, but in the Spirit, if so be that the Spirit of God dwell in you. Now if any man have not the Spirit of Christ, he is none of his.

10 And if Christ *be* in you, the body *is* dead because of sin; but the Spirit *is* life because of righteousness.

11 But if the Spirit of him that raised up Jesus from the dead dwell in you, he that raised up Christ from the dead shall also quicken your mortal bodies by his Spirit that dwelleth in you.

12 Therefore, brethren, we are debtors, not to the flesh, to live after the flesh.

13 For if ye live after the flesh, ye shall die: but if ye through the Spirit do mortify the deeds of the body, ye shall live.

14 For as many as are led by the Spirit of God, they are the sons of God.

15 For ye have not received the spirit of bondage again to fear; but ye have received the Spirit of adoption, whereby we cry, Abba, Father.

16 The Spirit itself beareth witness with our spirit, that we are the children of God:

17 And if children, then heirs; heirs of God, and joint-heirs with Christ; if so be that we suffer with *him*, that we may be also glorified together.

18 For I reckon that the sufferings of this present time *are* not worthy *to be compared* with the glory which shall be revealed in us.

19 For the earnest expectation of the creature waiteth for the manifestation of the sons of God.

20 For the creature was made subject to vanity, not willingly, but by reason of him who hath subjected *the same* in hope,

21 Because the creature itself also shall be delivered from the bondage of corruption into the glorious liberty of the children of God.

22 For we know that the whole creation groaneth and travaileth in pain together until now.

23 And not only *they*, but ourselves also, which have the firstfruits of the Spirit, even we ourselves groan within ourselves, waiting for the adoption, *to wit*, the redemption of our body.

24 For we are saved by hope: but hope that is seen is not hope: for what a man seeth, why doth he yet hope for?

25 But if we hope for that we see not, *then* do we with patience wait for *it*.

26 Likewise the Spirit also helpeth our infirmities: for we know not what we should pray for as we ought: but the Spirit itself maketh intercession for us with groanings which cannot be uttered.

27 And he that searcheth the hearts knoweth what *is* the mind of the Spirit, because he maketh intercession for the saints according to *the will of* God.

28 And we know that all things work together for good to them that love God, to them who are the called according to *his* purpose.

29 For whom he did foreknow, he also did predestinate *to be* conformed to the image of his Son, that he might be the firstborn among many brethren.

30 Moreover whom he did predestinate, them he also called: and whom he called, them he also justified: and whom he justified, them he also glorified.

31 What shall we then say to these things? If God *be* for us, who *can be* against us?

32 He that spared not his own Son, but delivered him up for us all, how shall he not with him also freely give us all things?

33 Who shall lay any thing to the charge of God's elect? *It is* God that justifieth.

34 Who *is* he that condemneth? *It is* Christ that died, yea rather, that is risen again, who is even at the right hand of God, who also maketh intercession for us.

35 Who shall separate us from the love of Christ? *shall* tribulation, or distress, or persecution, or famine, or nakedness, or peril, or sword?

36 As it is written, For thy sake we are killed all the day long; we are accounted as sheep for the slaughter.

37 Nay, in all these things we are more than conquerors through him that loved us.

38 For I am persuaded, that neither death, nor life, nor angels, nor principalities, nor powers, nor things present, nor things to come,

39 Nor height, nor depth, nor any other creature, shall be able to separate us from the love of God, which is in Christ Jesus our Lord.

CHAPTER 9

I SAY the truth in Christ, I lie not, my conscience also bearing me witness in the Holy Ghost,

2 That I have great heaviness and continual sorrow in my heart.

3 For I could wish that myself were accursed from Christ for my brethren, my kinsmen according to the flesh:

4 Who are Israelites; to whom *pertaineth* the adoption, and the glory, and the covenants, and the giving of the law, and the service *of God*, and the promises;

5 Whose *are* the fathers, and of whom as concerning the flesh Christ *came*, who is over all, God blessed for ever. Amen.

6 Not as though the word of God hath taken none effect. For they *are* not all Israel, which are of Israel:

7 Neither, because they are the seed of Abraham, *are they* all children: but, In Isaac shall thy seed be called.

8 That is, They which are the children of the flesh, these *are* not the children of God: but the

children of the promise are counted for the seed.

9 For this *is* the word of promise, At this time will I come, and Sara shall have a son.

10 And not only *this*, but when Rebecca also had conceived by one, *even* by our father Isaac;

11 (For *the children* being not yet born, neither having done any good or evil, that the purpose of God according to election might stand, not of works, but of him that calleth;)

12 It was said unto her, The elder shall serve the younger.

13 As it is written, Jacob have I loved, but Esau have I hated.

14 What shall we say then? *Is there* unrighteousness with God? God forbid.

15 For he saith to Moses, I will have mercy on whom I will have mercy, and I will have compassion on whom I will have compassion.

16 So then *it is* not of him that willeth, nor of him that runneth, but of God that sheweth mercy.

17 For the scripture saith unto Pharaoh, Even for this same purpose have I raised thee up, that I might shew my power in thee, and that my name might be declared throughout all the earth.

18 Therefore hath he mercy on whom he will *have mercy*, and whom he will he hardeneth.

19 Thou wilt say then unto me, Why doth he yet find fault? For who hath resisted his will?

20 Nay but, O man, who art thou that repliest against God? Shall the thing formed say to him that formed *it*, Why hast thou made me thus?

21 Hath not the potter power over the clay, of the same lump to make one vessel unto honour, and another unto dishonour?

22 *What* if God, willing to shew *his* wrath, and to make his power known, endured with much longsuffering the vessels of wrath fitted to destruction:

23 And that he might make known the riches of his glory on the vessels of mercy, which he had afore prepared unto glory,

24 Even us, whom he hath called, not of the Jews only, but also of the Gentiles?

25 As he saith also in Osee, I will call them my people, which were not my people; and her beloved, which was not beloved.

26 And it shall come to pass, *that* in the place where it was said unto them, Ye *are* not my people; there shall they be called the children of the living God.

27 Esaias also crieth concerning Israel, Though the number of the children of Israel be as the sand of the sea, a remnant shall be saved:

28 For he will finish the work, and cut *it* short in righteousness: because a short work will the Lord make upon the earth.

29 And as Esaias said before, Except the Lord of Sabaoth had left us a seed, we had been as Sodoma, and been made like unto Gomorrha.

30 What shall we say then? That the Gentiles, which followed not after righteousness, have attained to righteousness, even the righteousness which is of faith.

31 But Israel, which followed af-

ter the law of righteousness, hath not attained to the law of righteousness.

32 Wherefore? Because *they sought it* not by faith, but as it were by the works of the law. For they stumbled at that stumblingstone;

33 As it is written, Behold, I lay in Sion a stumblingstone and rock of offence: and whosoever believeth on him shall not be ashamed.

CHAPTER 10

BRETHREN, my heart's desire and prayer to God for Israel is, that they might be saved.

2 For I bear them record that they have a zeal of God, but not according to knowledge.

3 For they being ignorant of God's righteousness, and going about to establish their own righteousness, have not submitted themselves unto the righteousness of God.

4 For Christ *is* the end of the law for righteousness to every one that believeth.

5 For Moses describeth the righteousness which is of the law, That the man which doeth those things shall live by them.

6 But the righteousness which is of faith speaketh on this wise, Say not in thine heart, Who shall ascend into heaven? (that is, to bring Christ down *from above*:)

7 Or, Who shall descend into the deep? (that is, to bring up Christ again from the dead.)

8 But what saith it? The word is nigh thee, *even* in thy mouth, and in thy heart: that is, the word of faith, which we preach;

9 That if thou shalt confess with thy mouth the Lord Jesus, and shalt believe in thine heart that God hath raised him from the dead, thou shalt be saved.

10 For with the heart man believeth unto righteousness; and with the mouth confession is made unto salvation.

11 For the scripture saith, Whosoever believeth on him shall not be ashamed.

12 For there is no difference between the Jew and the Greek: for the same Lord over all is rich unto all that call upon him.

13 For whosoever shall call upon the name of the Lord shall be saved.

14 How then shall they call on him in whom they have not believed? and how shall they believe in him of whom they have not heard? and how shall they hear without a preacher?

15 And how shall they preach, except they be sent? as it is written, How beautiful are the feet of them that preach the gospel of peace, and bring glad tidings of good things!

16 But they have not all obeyed the gospel. For Esaias saith, Lord, who hath believed our report?

17 So then faith *cometh* by hearing, and hearing by the word of God.

18 But I say, Have they not heard? Yes verily, their sound went into all the earth, and their words unto the ends of the world.

19 But I say, Did not Israel know? First Moses saith, I will provoke you to jealousy by *them that are* no people, *and* by a foolish nation I will anger you.

20 But Esaias is very bold, and saith, I was found of them that sought me not; I was made manifest unto them that asked not after me.

21 But to Israel he saith, All day long I have stretched forth my hands unto a disobedient and gainsaying people.

CHAPTER 11

I SAY then, Hath God cast away his people? God forbid. For I also am an Israelite, of the seed of Abraham, *of* the tribe of Benjamin.

2 God hath not cast away his people which he foreknew. Wot ye not what the scripture saith of Elias? how he maketh intercession to God against Israel, saying,

3 Lord, they have killed thy prophets, and digged down thine altars; and I am left alone, and they seek my life.

4 But what saith the answer of God unto him? I have reserved to myself seven thousand men, who have not bowed the knee to *the image of* Baal.

5 Even so then at this present time also there is a remnant according to the election of grace.

6 And if by grace, then *is it* no more of works: otherwise grace is no more grace. But if *it be* of works, then is it no more grace: otherwise work is no more work.

7 What then? Israel hath not ob-

tained that which he seeketh for; but the election hath obtained it, and the rest were blinded

8 (According as it is written, God hath given them the spirit of slumber, eyes that they should not see, and ears that they should not hear;) unto this day.

9 And David saith, Let their table be made a snare, and a trap, and a stumblingblock, and a recompence unto them:

10 Let their eyes be darkened, that they may not see, and bow down their back alway.

11 I say then, Have they stumbled that they should fall? God forbid: but *rather* through their fall salvation *is come* unto the Gentiles, for to provoke them to jealousy.

12 Now if the fall of them *be* the riches of the world, and the diminishing of them the riches of the Gentiles; how much more their fulness?

13 For I speak to you Gentiles, inasmuch as I am the apostle of the Gentiles, I magnify mine office:

14 If by any means I may provoke to emulation *them which are* my flesh, and might save some of them.

15 For if the casting away of them *be* the reconciling of the world, what *shall* the receiving *of them be*, but life from the dead?

16 For if the firstfruit *be* holy, the lump *is* also *holy*: and if the root *be* holy, so *are* the branches.

17 And if some of the branches be broken off, and thou, being a wild olive tree, wert graffed in among them, and with them par-

takest of the root and fatness of the olive tree;

18 Boast not against the branches. But if thou boast, thou bearest not the root, but the root thee.

19 Thou wilt say then, The branches were broken off, that I might be graffed in.

20 Well; because of unbelief they were broken off, and thou standest by faith. Be not high-minded, but fear:

21 For if God spared not the natural branches, *take heed* lest he also spare not thee.

22 Behold therefore the goodness and severity of God: on them which fell, severity; but toward thee, goodness, if thou continue in *his* goodness: otherwise thou also shalt be cut off.

23 And they also, if they abide not still in unbelief, shall be graffed in: for God is able to graff them in again.

24 For if thou wert cut out of the olive tree which is wild by nature, and wert graffed contrary to nature into a good olive tree: how much more shall these, which be the natural *branches*, be graffed into their own olive tree?

25 For I would not, brethren, that ye should be ignorant of this mystery, lest ye should be wise in your own conceits; that blindness in part is happened to Israel, until the fulness of the Gentiles be come in.

26 And so all Israel shall be saved: as it is written, There shall come out of Sion the Deliverer, and shall turn away ungodliness from Jacob:

27 For this *is* my covenant unto them, when I shall take away their sins.

28 As concerning the gospel, *they are* enemies for your sakes: but as touching the election, *they are* beloved for the fathers' sakes.

29 For the gifts and calling of God *are* without repentance.

30 For as ye in times past have not believed God, yet have now obtained mercy through their unbelief:

31 Even so have these also now not believed, that through your mercy they also may obtain mercy.

32 For God hath concluded them all in unbelief, that he might have mercy upon all.

33 O the depth of the riches both of the wisdom and knowledge of God! how unsearchable *are* his judgments, and his ways past finding out!

34 For who hath known the mind of the Lord? or who hath been his counsellor?

35 Or who hath first given to him, and it shall be recompensed unto him again?

36 For of him, and through him, and to him, *are* all things: to whom *be* glory for ever. Amen.

CHAPTER 12

I BESEECH you therefore, brethren, by the mercies of God, that ye present your bodies a living sacrifice, holy, acceptable unto God, *which is* your reasonable service.

2 And be not conformed to this world: but be ye transformed by the renewing of your mind, that

ye may prove what *is* that good, and acceptable, and perfect, will of God.

3 For I say, through the grace given unto me, to every man that is among you, not to think *of himself* more highly than he ought to think; but to think soberly, according as God hath dealt to every man the measure of faith.

4 For as we have many members in one body, and all members have not the same office:

5 So we, *being* many, are one body in Christ, and every one members one of another.

6 Having then gifts differing according to the grace that is given to us, whether prophecy, *let us prophesy* according to the proportion of faith;

7 Or ministry, *let us wait* on *our* ministering: or he that teacheth, on teaching;

8 Or he that exhorteth, on exhortation: he that giveth, *let him do it* with simplicity; he that ruleth, with diligence; he that sheweth mercy, with cheerfulness.

9 *Let* love be without dissimulation. Abhor that which is evil; cleave to that which is good.

10 *Be* kindly affectioned one to another with brotherly love; in honour preferring one another;

11 Not slothful in business; fervent in spirit; serving the Lord;

12 Rejoicing in hope; patient in tribulation; continuing instant in prayer;

13 Distributing to the necessity of saints; given to hospitality.

14 Bless them which persecute you: bless, and curse not.

15 Rejoice with them that do rejoice, and weep with them that weep.

16 *Be* of the same mind one toward another. Mind not high things, but condescend to men of low estate. Be not wise in your own conceits.

17 Recompense to no man evil for evil. Provide things honest in the sight of all men.

18 If it be possible, as much as lieth in you, live peaceably with all men.

19 Dearly beloved, avenge not yourselves, but *rather* give place unto wrath: for it is written, Vengeance *is* mine; I will repay, saith the Lord.

20 Therefore if thine enemy hunger, feed him; if he thirst, give him drink: for in so doing thou shalt heap coals of fire on his head.

21 Be not overcome of evil, but overcome evil with good.

CHAPTER 13

LET every soul be subject unto the higher powers. For there is no power but of God: the powers that be are ordained of God.

2 Whosoever therefore resisteth the power, resisteth the ordinance of God: and they that resist shall receive to themselves damnation.

3 For rulers are not a terror to good works, but to the evil. Wilt thou then not be afraid of the power? do that which is good, and thou shalt have praise of the same:

4 For he is the minister of God to thee for good. But if thou do

that which is evil, be afraid; for he beareth not the sword in vain: for he is the minister of God, a revenger to *execute* wrath upon him that doeth evil.

5 Wherefore *ye* must needs be subject, not only for wrath, but also for conscience sake.

6 For for this cause pay ye tribute also: for they are God's ministers, attending continually upon this very thing.

7 Render therefore to all their dues: tribute to whom tribute *is due*; custom to whom custom; fear to whom fear; honour to whom honour.

8 Owe no man any thing, but to love one another: for he that loveth another hath fulfilled the law.

9 For this, Thou shalt not commit adultery, Thou shalt not kill, Thou shalt not steal, Thou shalt not bear false witness, Thou shalt not covet; and if *there be* any other commandment, it is briefly comprehended in this saying, namely, Thou shalt love thy neighbour as thyself.

10 Love worketh no ill to his neighbour: therefore love *is* the fulfilling of the law.

11 And that, knowing the time, that now *it is* high time to awake out of sleep: for now *is* our salvation nearer than when we believed.

12 The night is far spent, the day is at hand: let us therefore cast off the works of darkness, and let us put on the armour of light.

13 Let us walk honestly, as in the day; not in rioting and drunkenness, not in chambering and wantonness, not in strife and envying.

14 But put ye on the Lord Jesus Christ, and make not provision for the flesh, to *fulfil* the lusts *thereof*.

CHAPTER 14

HIM that is weak in the faith receive ye, *but* not to doubtful disputations.

2 For one believeth that he may eat all things: another, who is weak, eateth herbs.

3 Let not him that eateth despise him that eateth not; and let not him which eateth not judge him that eateth: for God hath received him.

4 Who art thou that judgest another man's servant? to his own master he standeth or falleth. Yea, he shall be holden up: for God is able to make him stand.

5 One man esteemeth one day above another: another esteemeth every day *alike*. Let every man be fully persuaded in his own mind.

6 He that regardeth the day, regardeth *it* unto the Lord; and he that regardeth not the day, to the Lord he doth not regard *it*. He that eateth, eateth to the Lord, for he giveth God thanks; and he that eateth not, to the Lord he eateth not, and giveth God thanks.

7 For none of us liveth to himself, and no man dieth to himself.

8 For whether we live, we live unto the Lord; and whether we die, we die unto the Lord:

whether we live therefore, or die, we are the Lord's.

9 For to this end Christ both died, and rose, and revived, that he might be Lord both of the dead and living.

10 But why dost thou judge thy brother? or why dost thou set at nought thy brother? for we shall all stand before the judgment seat of Christ.

11 For it is written, *As* I live, saith the Lord, every knee shall bow to me, and every tongue shall confess to God.

12 So then every one of us shall give account of himself to God.

13 Let us not therefore judge one another any more: but judge this rather, that no man put a stumblingblock or an occasion to fall in *his* brother's way.

14 I know, and am persuaded by the Lord Jesus, that *there is* nothing unclean of itself: but to him that esteemeth any thing to be unclean, to him *it is* unclean.

15 But if thy brother be grieved with *thy* meat, now walkest thou not charitably. Destroy not him with thy meat, for whom Christ died.

16 Let not then your good be evil spoken of:

17 For the kingdom of God is not meat and drink; but righteousness, and peace, and joy in the Holy Ghost.

18 For he that in these things serveth Christ *is* acceptable to God, and approved of men.

19 Let us therefore follow after the things which make for peace, and things wherewith one may edify another.

20 For meat destroy not the work of God. All things indeed *are* pure; but *it is* evil for that man who eateth with offence.

21 *It is* good neither to eat flesh, nor to drink wine, nor *any thing* whereby thy brother stumbleth, or is offended, or is made weak.

22 Hast thou faith? have *it* to thyself before God. Happy *is* he that condemneth not himself in that thing which he alloweth.

23 And he that doubteth is damned if he eat, because *he eateth* not of faith: for whatsoever *is* not of faith is sin.

CHAPTER 15

WE then that are strong ought to bear the infirmities of the weak, and not to please ourselves.

2 Let every one of us please *his* neighbour for *his* good to edification.

3 For even Christ pleased not himself; but, as it is written, The reproaches of them that reproached thee fell on me.

4 For whatsoever things were written aforetime were written for our learning, that we through patience and comfort of the scriptures might have hope.

5 Now the God of patience and consolation grant you to be likeminded one toward another according to Christ Jesus:

6 That ye may with one mind *and* one mouth glorify God, even the Father of our Lord Jesus Christ.

7 Wherefore receive ye one another, as Christ also received us to the glory of God.

8 Now I say that Jesus Christ was

a minister of the circumcision for the truth of God, to confirm the promises *made* unto the fathers:

9 And that the Gentiles might glorify God for *his* mercy; as it is written, For this cause I will confess to thee among the Gentiles, and sing unto thy name.

10 And again he saith, Rejoice, ye Gentiles, with his people.

11 And again, Praise the Lord, all ye Gentiles; and laud him, all ye people.

12 And again, Esaias saith, There shall be a root of Jesse, and he that shall rise to reign over the Gentiles; in him shall the Gentiles trust.

13 Now the God of hope fill you with all joy and peace in believing, that ye may abound in hope, through the power of the Holy Ghost.

14 And I myself also am persuaded of you, my brethren, that ye also are full of goodness, filled with all knowledge, able also to admonish one another.

15 Nevertheless, brethren, I have written the more boldly unto you in some sort, as putting you in mind, because of the grace that is given to me of God,

16 That I should be the minister of Jesus Christ to the Gentiles, ministering the gospel of God, that the offering up of the Gentiles might be acceptable, being sanctified by the Holy Ghost.

17 I have therefore whereof I may glory through Jesus Christ in those things which pertain to God.

18 For I will not dare to speak of any of those things which Christ hath not wrought by me, to make the Gentiles obedient, by word and deed,

19 Through mighty signs and wonders, by the power of the Spirit of God; so that from Jerusalem, and round about unto Illyricum, I have fully preached the gospel of Christ.

20 Yea, so have I strived to preach the gospel, not where Christ was named, lest I should build upon another man's foundation:

21 But as it is written, To whom he was not spoken of, they shall see: and they that have not heard shall understand.

22 For which cause also I have been much hindered from coming to you.

23 But now having no more place in these parts, and having a great desire these many years to come unto you;

24 Whensoever I take my journey into Spain, I will come to you: for I trust to see you in my journey, and to be brought on my way thitherward by you, if first I be somewhat filled with your *company.*

25 But now I go unto Jerusalem to minister unto the saints.

26 For it hath pleased them of Macedonia and Achaia to make a certain contribution for the poor saints which are at Jerusalem.

27 It hath pleased them verily; and their debtors they are. For if the Gentiles have been made partakers of their spiritual things, their duty is also to minister unto them in carnal things.

28 When therefore I have performed this, and have sealed to

them this fruit, I will come by you into Spain.

29 And I am sure that, when I come unto you, I shall come in the fulness of the blessing of the gospel of Christ.

30 Now I beseech you, brethren, for the Lord Jesus Christ's sake, and for the love of the Spirit, that ye strive together with me in *your* prayers to God for me;

31 That I may be delivered from them that do not believe in Judaea; and that my service which *I have* for Jerusalem may be accepted of the saints;

32 That I may come unto you with joy by the will of God, and may with you be refreshed.

33 Now the God of peace *be* with you all. Amen.

CHAPTER 16

I COMMEND unto you Phebe our sister, which is a servant of the church which is at Cenchrea:

2 That ye receive her in the Lord, as becometh saints, and that ye assist her in whatsoever business she hath need of you: for she hath been a succourer of many, and of myself also.

3 Greet Priscilla and Aquila my helpers in Christ Jesus:

4 Who have for my life laid down their own necks: unto whom not only I give thanks, but also all the churches of the Gentiles.

5 Likewise *greet* the church that is in their house. Salute my well-beloved Epaenetus, who is the firstfruits of Achaia unto Christ.

6 Greet Mary, who bestowed much labour on us.

7 Salute Andronicus and Junia, my kinsmen, and my fellowprisoners, who are of note among the apostles, who also were in Christ before me.

8 Greet Amplias my beloved in the Lord.

9 Salute Urbane, our helper in Christ, and Stachys my beloved.

10 Salute Apelles approved in Christ. Salute them which are of Aristobulus' *household*.

11 Salute Herodion my kinsman. Greet them that be of the *household* of Narcissus, which are in the Lord.

12 Salute Tryphena and Tryphosa, who labour in the Lord. Salute the beloved Persis, which laboured much in the Lord.

13 Salute Rufus chosen in the Lord, and his mother and mine.

14 Salute Asyncritus, Phlegon, Hermas, Patrobas, Hermes, and the brethren which are with them.

15 Salute Philologus, and Julia, Nereus, and his sister, and Olympas, and all the saints which are with them.

16 Salute one another with an holy kiss. The churches of Christ salute you.

17 Now I beseech you, brethren, mark them which cause divisions and offences contrary to the doctrine which ye have learned; and avoid them.

18 For they that are such serve not our Lord Jesus Christ, but their own belly; and by good words and fair speeches deceive the hearts of the simple.

19 For your obedience is come abroad unto all *men*. I am glad

therefore on your behalf: but yet I would have you wise unto that which is good, and simple concerning evil.

20 And the God of peace shall bruise Satan under your feet shortly. The grace of our Lord Jesus Christ *be* with you. Amen.

21 Timotheus my workfellow, and Lucius, and Jason, and Sosipater, my kinsmen, salute you.

22 I Tertius, who wrote *this* epistle, salute you in the Lord.

23 Gaius mine host, and of the whole church, saluteth you. Erastus the chamberlain of the city saluteth you, and Quartus a brother.

24 The grace of our Lord Jesus Christ *be* with you all. Amen.

25 Now to him that is of power to stablish you according to my gospel, and the preaching of Jesus Christ, according to the revelation of the mystery, which was kept secret since the world began,

26 But now is made manifest, and by the scriptures of the prophets, according to the commandment of the everlasting God, made known to all nations for the obedience of faith:

27 To God only wise, *be* glory through Jesus Christ for ever. Amen.

¶ Written to the Romans from Corinthus, and sent by Phebe servant of the church at Cenchrea.

Grady Publications would like to thank Bearing Precious Seed of Lansing, Michigan, for supplying the formatted text for the books of John and Romans.